The Teacher Aide in the Instructional Team

the teacher aide
in the instructional team

Don A. Welty
Director of Continuing Education
College of the Desert

Dorothy R. Welty
Elementary Teacher
Rancho Mirage Elementary School

Gregg Division/McGraw-Hill Book Company

New York St. Louis Dallas San Francisco Auckland Düsseldorf
Johannesburg Kuala Lumpur London Mexico Montreal New Delhi
Panama Paris São Paulo Singapore Sydney Tokyo Toronto

Library of Congress Cataloging in Publication Data

Welty, Don A
    The teacher aide in the instructional team.

    Includes bibliographical references and index.
    1. Teachers' assistants.   2.   Teaching—Aids and
devices.   I.   Welty, Dorothy R., joint author.
II.   Title.
LB2844.1. A8W44   371.1'412   75-37844
ISBN 0-07-069263-7

All the chapter opening illustrations
were drawn by Christopher Giamo, age four.

The Teacher Aide in the Instructional Team

1234567890 KPKP 7832109876

The editors for this book were Carole O'Keefe and
Zivile K. Khoury, the designer was Tracy A. Glasner,
and the production supervisor was Phyllis D. Lemkowitz.
It was set in Caledonia by Progressive Typographers.
Printed and bound by Kingsport Press, Inc.

To our four sons,
Bill, John, Dick, and Bob

contents

CHAPTER 4   Mathematics

CHAPTER 5   Creative Arts

**CHAPTER 6   Playground Supervision,
                       Equipment, and Activities**

CHAPTER 7   Instructional Media

preface

It is exciting to see a new vocation developing, and even more so when that vocation permits an upgrading of a whole profession. This is what is happening to the teaching profession, through the growing acceptance by school districts of the employment of instructional aides as part of the staff.

It is surprising that this staffing plan has taken such a long time to develop. Other professionals, such as doctors, lawyers, dentists, and architects, have long realized that their jobs included some tasks which did not require their professional expertise; these duties were then delegated to someone who had been trained to do them.

For some reason, teachers, until very recently, felt the whole job of teaching was theirs alone. They patiently graded all papers, filled in all forms, typed all worksheets, cleaned all cupboards, supervised all play periods, and then felt guilty because they could not find time to diagnose and study the child's needs and develop a learning plan to fulfill those needs. Now that trained instructional aides are beginning to regularly assume duties in the classroom, teachers are able to respond to their duties more effectively and to teach more competently than they have ever done before.

Nurses' assistants, dental technicians, draftsmen, and other professionals' assistants have gone through a training program to gain necessary on-the-job skills. The educational profession is just now forming training programs for the instructional aide. When instructional aide programs were first organized, instructors assumed that because all people go to school at some time, adults would somehow be automatically prepared to help in a classroom. This, of course, resulted in teachers having to take classroom time to train aides; the aides in turn were disillusioned with the job because they did not understand either their role or the changes that had occurred since they went to school.

Many schools then began to offer aides a short course on *how* to be a teacher's aide, but it soon became obvious that one short course would not answer the need. Now, most post-high school institutions offer one- or two-year programs to prepare the aide for the position. Sometimes, different training programs provide different titles for the trainee, such as *aide, associate, assistant,* and so on. As instructors began to develop a variety of courses for aides, they realized that they had to search frantically for materials for their students. Many instructors used teacher-training books and adapted them for the aide-training course. But the position of instructional aide is most certainly *not* a watered down teaching job; thus, this ap-

proach was totally unsuccessful. What has long been needed is
material written especially for the instruction of the aide. That is
the purpose of this book: to provide the student-aide with a broad
picture of the aide's role in the school system, and to give relevant
background and information on ways to work within important curriculum areas.

To feel comfortable in the educational environment, an aide
must be familiar with other school personnel and with the mechanics
of the school plant. When this familiarity has been achieved, students will also have a better idea of how their position fits into the
overall picture. There are some techniques and attitudes which will
help aides to function more comfortably and effectively, such as understanding the chain of command, respecting confidentiality, and
knowing where help can be obtained, how to help others, what the
delegated duties are, and what responsibilities are specifically limited to the teacher. If the aide knows what qualities the schools
are looking for when they hire and how they can help themselves to
improve their skills and competencies, the aide will be of more value
to the team. Innate talents must be brought to the job, and the aide
will want to develop these talents further. Essential skills must be
developed, and the aide will need the help of supervising teachers,
and formal courses, and professional literature. One of the most important of these skills is the ability to work successfully with children. Although we have all been children at one time and may have
children of our own, and know we have some talent at working with
them, we all feel the need for some direct help and suggestion. The
first chapter of this book touches on all these points, though not in
detail, as each of these topics have been written about extensively
elsewhere; but a broad picture is nevertheless presented. The list of
suggested references has been carefully studied and is offered to the
reader as a source of additional help.

One of the first duties that an aide is often given (and for many
aides the only responsibility) is playground and lunchroom supervision. This job should consist of more than standing on the playground with a whistle ready to blow every time a child commits an
infraction of the rules, or of acting as a disciplinary guard over the
eating area. An aide who comes to the playground or to the lunch
area with a knowledge of where the children are—emotionally,
physically, socially—and who has some familiarity with various
equipment, the rules of many games, techniques of working with
and encouraging children, and a practical knowledge of first aid as

well as a firm yet pleasant attitude, can turn a playground, physical education area, or lunchroom from a field of potential conflict to an area where children can grow and learn.

Communication skills include speaking, listening, reading, and writing, and these are perhaps the major academic obligations the schools have. The jobs in this area are limited only by the aide's skills, knowledge, and imagination. This text provides some needed background knowledge, methods, and suggestions on how to be effective in a good language arts class.

Social sciences and science are some important areas of learning that offer opportunities for the schools to help children learn to think. Aides need some basic skills in both areas; in the chapter dealing with these subjects, the text provides a description of necessary skills and suggestions for ways to apply them in the classroom.

"New" math can be as much fun for grownups as it is for children. The only requirement for working successfully with the new math is that one needs to learn the vocabulary and understand the approach. The chapter on math presents many ways of correlating "new" and "old" math.

The treatment of the creative arts in the text is not limited to lists of materials, suggestions for playing the piano, or advice on cleaning up. It is necessary for the aide to understand that creativity is more than being able to paint a beautiful picture or compose a song. Creativity includes searching, organizing, discovering, originating, and communicating. Schools and their personnel need to provide not only skills but also freedom for children.

One of the causes of recent changes in education the explosion of knowledge, improved skill-building techniques, the relevancy and immediate availability of information—is the increase and constant improvement of audiovisual equipment used in schools. Of course, these machines and aids are useless unless there is a person trained to use them, gather materials to implement them, and provide a good learning environment for them. The chapter on audiovisual aids presents both skills for using the aids and suggestions for preparing, presenting, and evaluating their usefulness.

There are various types of aide positions within the educational field. Some aides are assigned only to secretarial or playground supervision jobs. Some aides work with preschoolers, while others work at various other levels, including college. Some aides work with specialized groups of children, such as the physically handicapped, mentally handicapped, emotionally handicapped, or gifted

children. Although this book was written mainly for the instructional aide in the regular elementary school classroom, aides in other
positions will find the information helpful.

The position of teacher aide is a new concept—the training requirements, responsibilities, and the training programs are varied.
The position has not yet been defined with any uniformity, but this
will surely happen in the future. Already many schools consider the
aide position as much a part of the total personnel as the teacher, the
secretary, etc. Such schools have developed a careful screening procedure, require thorough training, and have come to an agreement
on the responsibilities of the aide. They are now seeing that aides
are given the status their position deserves. This is going to happen
more and more frequently. This book has been written to smooth
the way for the implementation of this view of the teacher aide.

Grateful acknowledgment and appreciation are expressed to Dr.
Darwyn Vickers for his constant encouragement and assistance and
to Dorothy Swartz for her typing and retyping. A very special thank
you to the teachers and aides who have worked with us, serving as
sounding boards for our ideas and plans.

Don A. Welty
Dorothy R. Welty

foreword

As the age of the average American citizen becomes increasingly younger with each passing year, there is a like increase in the demand for a mass educational system to include the techniques of both rapid change and a more individualized instruction brought about by closer teacher/pupil relationships. This double-edged growth—the increase in the numbers of students at all levels and the changing curriculum—is placing an unparalleled burden on education from the operation and maintenance of the school buildings to employee salaries.

Coming at an opportune time, *The Teacher Aide in the Instructional Team* offers a solid solution to these financial problems. Instructional aides (paraprofessionals) are a new and effective source of labor, assisting in the job of educating at a cost one-third that of the classroom teacher. Recognized as a productive solution, the instructional aides have been integrated into many school systems nationally and are being considered in many more.

This solution, however, has a twofold demand: the instructional aide needs to be trained to insure necessary pupil progress, and the classroom teacher and school administrator require training to use this new educational resource.

Instructional aides are high school and college students as well as interested parents and citizens exploring the profession as a career vehicle. Administrators of today's public and private schools are demonstrating that using the paraprofessional is a great asset to students.

Until now there has been no adequate guide or text to throw light on the complexities inherent in the manifold skills and body of knowledge necessary to effectively aid the pupil. The authors' experience and expertise as teachers, administrators, and pioneers in the field of instructional aide training, from the elementary to the college level, establishes on a sound and practical footing the data presented. They have gone beyond their extensive experiences to include a body of research which is rich and current. The dialogue and syntax are beautifully stated in a manner which readily reaches and helps the reader. Parents will also find the background, content, and suggestions readable and functional.

The Doctors Welty, having experienced the needs of recruiting, training, and supervising paraprofessionals, purposefully graduated their text to serve not only the instructional aide and parent, but those educators with whom the aide works. Administrators and teachers will acclaim this text as a key reference for their paraprofessional staff.

Darwyne Vickers, Ed.D.
Director, Certificated Personnel
Palm Springs Unified School District
Palm Springs, California

The Teacher Aide in the Instructional Team

Introduction

A brand new vocation is making a big impact on the educational world. It is so new that the requirements, the training, and even the job description have not been totally agreed upon. In fact, it is not even universally agreed upon that such a vocational need exists. But each year there is a greater demand for the service and a larger offering of ways to satisfy it. The vocation is that of the teacher aide in the public school.

Aides in the elementary classroom come from a large variety of backgrounds. Age may vary from teenagers who have free time and want to work with children, to grandparents who not only extend help in academic areas but frequently offer laps to hold the very young and stories to tell. Aides come from all economic and social backgrounds. Some aides have only a

the aide 1

grade school education, and others have advanced degrees. They may be men or women, from all walks of life, all races, and all creeds. The one thing they should have in common is that they like to be around children and want to help them. Otherwise they would do better to seek another field of employment or volunteer service.

The pay scale for aides is not high, so they must be attracted to the job for other reasons. For instance, students just out of high school may work as aides for a year. They may be thinking seriously of becoming teachers but aren't quite sure that they are interested in education. An excellent way to find out is to get classroom experience as an aide. By watching an experienced teacher work and being in touch with school curricula, they will have a better idea of how they relate to children as well as to the established modes of educating the young.

Many parents miss the companionship of their own children who are grown and find the association with school children satisfying. Some parents with school-age children need to work for added income. They may not want the responsibility of a full-time job or else they cannot take all day away from their home duties, so they work several hours a day as an aide. This job provides the same schedule as their children's, and even the same vacations. An important fringe benefit is that they also have a better idea of the educational process in which their children are involved.

The role of aides is as different as their backgrounds. Some aides spend all their time at school supervising on the playground. Others aid the teachers, but do not work directly with children. Their assignments may be typing, filing and keeping records, preparing classroom materials, and housekeeping duties. Although they are very helpful to the teacher, in many instances the children are not aware of their presence. However, usually the aide works directly with the children, in small groups or on a one-to-one tutoring basis. In so doing, the aide is definitely a member of the child's circle of adult friends. Some aides are very specialized and work only in certain areas of the school or the curriculum. Examples of these may be aides who work with remedial reading teachers, music or art aides, library aides, special-class aides who work with gifted or mentally and physically handicapped children, and many others. The growing trend is to include aides in a teaching team which is made up of a differentiated staff, that is, a teaching staff which includes personnel other then certified teachers. This role carries with it very definite responsibilities and will be discussed later in this chapter.

As the role of the aide comes into clearer focus, school systems set up the general requirements and specific training they want their aides to have. Some schools ask only that the candidate like children. At the other end of the scale, some schools require their aides to have an associate of arts degree. Both of these are extremes. The median requirement is that the aide candidate hold a high school diploma. However, it should be noted here that as more community colleges develop one-year certificate and two-year A.A. degree programs, more schools will require one of these as a condition of employment.

The School System

If you are going to become a part of the school district, you should know how the system is organized, who the people in the system are, and how you and your job fit into its framework.

Typical organization of a school district.

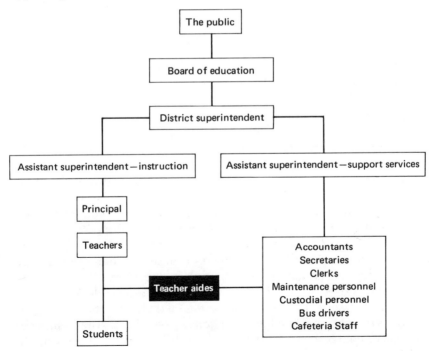

At the top of the school system you will find the *people*. The people—or public—approve bond issues and override taxes. In some states the school budget must be taken to the people to be adopted. The public elects and can recall the district's board members. The people are welcome to attend the school board meetings and can take part in the meeting either by asking to be on the agenda or by responding to an invitation to speak.

The *board of education* is made up of lay people who have the responsibility for adopting policies, approving budgets, and approving bills. To help them with these responsibilities, a legal counsel is chosen which acts as a legal adviser to the board and prepares legal documents. In addition, the board has the services of the clerk of the board. The *clerk of the board* records the board's proceedings and handles the board's correspondence. The position of the board member is an elected and unsalaried one.

Directly below the board of education is the *office of the superintendent of schools*. The superintendent approves all expenditures and payrolls, interprets board policy, recommends all appointments, recommends budget and purchases, and approves proposed instruction and curriculum programs. The superintendent's range of duties is extremely broad, so the assistance of many people is needed. The number of assistants varies according to the size of the district. There are usually assistant superintendents in charge of instruction and in charge of support services.

The *assistant superintendent in charge of instruction* has a responsibility for special educators such as coordinators of music, art, athletics, health, and library. In addition to being responsible for instruction and curriculum, the assistant superintendent works with the individual schools through the school principal.

The school *principal* is middle management between the district administration and the local building staff. The principal assigns, schedules, guides, and evaluates the staff, and is responsible for everything that goes on in the school building. The staff usually includes teachers, aides, clerks, custodians, and food service people.

The *assistant superintendent in charge of support services* is responsible for all fiscal matters for the maintenance and operations of the schools, as well as the cafeteria and transportation departments. The assistant superintendent also supervises all classified or uncredentialed personnel in the district. The aides, clerks, custodians, and food service people take some of their directions from the school principal and teachers and some from the assistant superintendent in charge of support services or from people chosen by the assistant superintendent.

It is important that anyone working for the schools knows what the hierarchy is and follows it when seeking advice or help. The teacher aide should first go to the supervising teacher if there is a problem. If the problem cannot be resolved at that level, then it will be taken to the school principal. From there it will go to the person in the district office in charge of the department serving classified personnel.

The process of educating children is probably the most important business which is going on in your community. It takes many different kinds of people skilled in many different fields to do the job well. The job is done better and more efficiently when the people know their job and carry it out to the best of their ability.

The Changing World of Education

The educational world is an interesting and exciting one right now. Change is occurring just as in every other part of our society. The role of the educator, the role of the pupil, and even the role of the parent have been greatly affected by change. The causes for the change are many. Such things as the awareness for the need of educational reform, the knowledge explosion, technological advancement, the financial picture, and the knowledge of how children learn, all play an important part in bringing about this change.

Changes have shown up in curriculum, methods, buildings, school organization, and personnel. Every school reflects change; for some it is a minimum amount, probably brought about more by equipment and materials than by personnel or philosophy. For others, the changes indicate a very dedicated effort on the part of the whole school community to improve the school program. As an aide, you will be a part of changes in education. It will help you to know about the new trends in education.

Your role as an aide in the school is part of a new plan, that of differentiated staffing. We explained earlier that a differentiated staff is a teaching staff which is made up not only of certified teachers, but also of other personnel.

Team teaching is part of the differentiated staffing plan. In a team plan the staff may include clerks, aides, educational technicians, academic assistants, intern teachers, staff teachers, senior teachers, and master teachers. The requirements, responsibilities, and salaries increase at each level. The differentiation does not come about because one member is better that the other, but because they perform different tasks.

Some advantages of team teaching are:

1. Better use of teacher talents
2. More flexible pupil groupings
3. More efficient use of resources
4. Ease in training personnel such as beginning teachers, intern teachers, and aides, and in incorporating them into the program.
5. Greater sharing of ideas and methods among the team members
6. Greater chance of matching teaching techniques to the child's needs[1]

If a school is set up on the team plan, there may be some hierarchy in the team organization. Some teams have a strong master teacher as a team leader. Usually a team leader is selected because of above-average, if not superior, talents as a teacher, particular teaching strength, unusual ability in curriculum planning, skills in group leadership, and willingness to take on the responsibility of the team leader's role. The leader must serve not only as a member of the regular teaching team, but also as the team's coordinator and general manager.[2]

The team will also include a teacher with probably the same amount of teaching talents as the leader, but, instead of the leadership talents, the teacher will probably have skills in a special area such as research, writing learning packages, or taking some responsibility for in-service training.

The team may also include an apprentice or intern teacher who may be doing practice teaching or serving internship to satisfy requirements for certification. Intern teachers will be full, participating members of the team and will be involved in diagnosis and planning.

In a true team plan, all members are involved in the three phases of teaching: planning, implementing, and evaluating the results. As an aide, you will not be involved to the same extent as the teachers, but it will be helpful to you and the team if you participate in formulating objectives, are aware of the teaching plan, and take part in the evaluation sessions.

One of the requirements of team teaching is that the team has planning sessions. Preferably, the schedule should be such that it includes a daily planning time. If this is not possible, there must be

---

[1] Anderson, Robert H. *Teaching in a World of Change*, New York: Harcourt, Brace and World, Inc., 1966, p. 89.

[2] Ibid., p. 86.

Both teachers and aides participate in team teaching planning sessions. During these sessions the members of the
team discuss the day's or week's objectives and the ways of
accomplishing these objectives.

a time set aside at least once a week. The planning session should
be a time when the team sets the objective and the time, place,
methods, and materials needed to accomplish the objective. This
is actually when the set of directions is formulated and explained by
and to the team. The aide should be included in planning sessions
in order to have the opportunity to become fully aware of his or her
role. If you, as an aide, do not fully understand what is going on or
what is going to take place, ask for an explanation. Remember,
working relationships between aides and teachers are best when
both understand the objectives and the procedures required to reach
them.

Team teaching is often used in a new type of school setup, the
continuous progress or nongraded school structure. Before you
learn what a nongraded school structure is, you should first understand what the traditional graded school plan is.

The graded school is separated into several different grades.
Each grade is responsible for a certain part of the overall curriculum.
For instance, children may be taught cursive writing in third grade,
American history in the fifth grade, fractional numbers in the early
part of the sixth grade, and decimals in the later part. Children are

assigned to grade levels according to their age or date of birth. The *grade level* is the focal point. Curriculum is planned for grade levels, books are written for grade levels, and teachers are trained to teach at certain grade levels. Educators are now beginning to see that a child will not always fit into a certain chosen grade level just because he or she is of a given age. Some children find it impossible to accomplish one grade level's work in a year's time. Others can complete the work in less time. Because of these individual differences, the nongraded school, or continuous progress school, came into being.

Nongraded schools are organized in a different way from graded schools. In nongraded schools, grade levels do not exist. Children are not grouped according to their age. Instead, groups are flexible and change depending on a particular situation and the needs of the individual child. The way children are organized into groups is not the only difference between the two types of schools. The philosophy which guides the behavior of the staff toward the children differs. The *individual child* is the focal point in the nongraded school.

The following are the major aspects of the nongraded school:

1. Grade levels and the promotion-or-failure system do not exist. Instead, children are placed into flexible groups which meet both the needs of the individual child and of the group.
2. Groups are flexible enough so that children regularly come into contact both with other children of similar abilities and with other children of different abilities.
3. The curriculum is also flexible so that it can fit the child's individual needs.
4. Because of the flexible school organization, a wide variety of materials and instructional approaches which are based on the learning needs of the individual child are available.
5. Children are not graded A to F as they are in graded schools. Instead the evaluation of the child is individual.
6. Children learn at their own rate. They are not put under too much pressure if they are slow learners. But they are not bored if they are fast learners.

The teacher's role in the nongraded school is a more demanding one in terms of time and skills. To fit this new role, a teacher must be relieved of some former duties. The best way for this to happen is to have an aide in the classroom who can take over some of the load.

Reams of material in great variety are needed in this plan, and they must be well organized. The aide may be asked to gather the materials, to use them with the children, and then to keep them in good shape and available for future use in the class.

Some kind of record keeping will have to be developed to keep track of each child's growth and needs. Record keeping can be a very time-consuming task. The teacher will be more than happy to have an aide who is able to take over that job.

The reporting system usually includes a conference of parent and teacher, which sometimes includes the child. Often the teacher likes to reinforce comments by showing some of the child's work. This is easy to do if each child has a folder where some of the child's more pertinent papers have been placed. The teacher will choose the papers to include in each folder, but the aide can help by setting up the folders, filing the papers, and being alert to any recorded information which may be of value to the teacher. Parent conferences are an important tie between home and school. If the aide has some information gathered from working with the child which might be of value during the conference, it is important that it be shared with the teacher before the conference. Aides usually do not sit in on or join parent-teacher conferences unless the teacher specifically asks them to join. These are only a few suggestions of the many ways in which the aide can help in this plan.

The philosophy of the continuous progress plan can be summarized: In the continuous progress plan the staff does not gear teaching techniques to the book, grade level, or majority of children. Instead the techniques are geared to each child and his or her individual needs. A child is not grouped only with children of his or her age or grade level. Instead the child is put with children who have the same needs and are ready to reach similar goals, regardless of age. This plan calls for a clear focus on each child, on thoughtful diagnosing, on careful prescribing, and much individual work. It is no wonder the aide assumes an important role in the plan.

If the staff is committed to team teaching and the continuous progress plan, any available school space can be used. However, the program may be hampered by the inflexibility of space in a traditional school building. In the past, schools were built with *egg-crate classrooms*, that is, identically sized and shaped rooms opening off a central hallway. It was up to educators to plan programs which would fit into that type of structure. The trend now is to plan the program first, and then construct the building to reflect the needs of the program.

Naturally, with this kind of process, school plans will vary a great deal, but there are some elements common to new school structures.

One of the common plans is the *open-space classroom.* In this plan there is room for large-group presentations, space for various sizes of smaller groups, room for resource areas, special project areas, learning centers, teacher and aide stations, listening centers, and other imaginative ways to use the space. Here, furniture is movable, carpeting is frequently installed, and electrical plugs are scattered throughout the space so that audiovisual equipment can be used. Here students can be given the freedom of making choices as to what is the best kind of learning situation for them individually and what materials they will need for the learning activity.

In an open-space classroom children may choose to use audiovisual materials in a learning situation. Listening centers may be set up for this purpose.

Another common plan educators would like to have in their new school plant is a resource center—a very well equipped library—located physically so close to the classroom that it is really an extension of it. With the large choice of instructional media now available, pupils need the resource center close enough for practical use.

Frequently the school staff feels that all new schools should include specific space for the team. The team needs a planning space, a workroom, and a conference area.

The open-space concept frightens some teachers, aides, and parents. They are concerned about noise and the seeming lack of control because they see children moving around and many different groups talking at one time. This is not the problem it appears to be. Children become accustomed to the movement and are not disturbed by it. They appreciate the freedom to move around and get materials they need when they need them. Noise does not as a rule bother children. They, probably better than adults, can mentally shut out what they are not concerned with hearing. How many times have you observed a child totally engrossed in a TV program in a room where several other people are talking? And how many times have you eaten in a restaurant, seated next to another group of people, and were so engrossed with the conversation going on at your table that you had no idea of happenings or conversations at the other table?

The open-space classroom allows for more individualized learning opportunities and more team cooperation and sharing. As our educational programs move toward these objectives, more innovations in buildings and facilities will appear.

When educators began doing away with rigid school programs, the schools' schedules became another target for change. As new schools began to develop their schedules, they discovered that a schedule cannot be a fixed plan for a program to fit into. The program must first be planned, and the schedule must then be flexible enough to fit the program. This is the meaning of flexible scheduling.

Perhaps you can better understand the need for flexible scheduling if you think about your own day. Not every task takes the same amount of time. Some days, parts of tasks can be completely skipped. Some tasks require more preparation than others. In the time it takes to gather the equipment and materials for one task, another could be completed. If you tried to set your own day as rigidly as the students' school day has been set, you would not be able to complete many projects and you would waste time. Under a rigid school schedule the students experience the same frustrating results. In the drive for individualization and flexibility, the same innovative thinking about the schedule must be included.

Another trend in American education, especially in elementary education, is the move toward informal classrooms. The informal classroom plans are also called free schools, open classrooms, or free structures. They are usually patterned after the Infant Schools in England. One of the basic parts of the informal classroom plan is that children are allowed to make choices, varying from when they will come to school to choosing what materials they will use to get a required assignment done. In most cases, children have some say in planning their schedule, mapping their learning plan, and choosing the methods and materials they will use. The teacher's role changes from the fountain of information (which is impossible to fulfill) to a facilitator for learning. Perhaps the most important part of this plan, other than the children and adults themselves, is the environment the child works and plays in. There must be a richness of concrete materials which challenge a child to discover the *why* and *how*. The classroom climate is an accepting, encouraging, and warm one. Children are busy and happy. Teachers' and aides' tasks are numerous. What a challenge for the team! Both aides and teachers must be on their toes constantly, ready to give individual and group help on a great variety of experiences. They must be alert to the types of materials which will allow children to find answers. They must, somehow, keep track of the child's academic and psychological needs.

As we look over the changes which are taking place in education, it becomes obvious that schools are becoming more aware of the individual differences in children, and are developing ways to handle these differences.

Children are individuals. They differ in many ways: in physical and motor development, in emotional and social development, in rates of maturation and maturity levels, in social demands, in personal objectives, and in learning styles, to name only a few. It is becoming more obvious to educators that what works for one child may not work for another. The school owes each child a good education, not just the child who fits into a preconceived pattern. Therefore, if the changes necessary to accommodate these differences, whether in the school building plan, the daily schedule, a differentiated staff, or an open program, are to help children learn more efficiently, then it is necessary that all people involved in the changes do all they can to make them successful. If these changes are new to you, read about them, study them, and if there is an opportunity, visit a school where some of these ideas are used. These changes are based on careful consideration of how children learn best. The information you gain from them will be helpful in whatever school situation you are working.

You—The Aide

Aides are usually recruited in one of three ways. The school may advertise an opening. The prospective aide may call the school for information on how to apply. The school may ask the community colleges to send them applicants from their aide classes.

Usually, before you are selected for the job, you will have to fill out an application form, take a test, and go for an interview. The application form differs in each school, but usually it asks for general information and gives you some opportunity to let the school know why you are interested in this particular position. A sample application form is shown below. The test will be designed to provide data relevant to your academic preparations, special talents, interests, limitations, and strengths. The interview may be with the principal only, the teacher, a teaching team and the principal, a district personnel director, or a district screening committee. The interviewer may only ask questions *about* you, but more often will ask

TEACHER AIDE APPLICATION FORM

Name _____ Date of birth _____ Sex ____ Marital status____

Address_____ Dependents (age and relationship) _____

Highest grade completed _____

Typing speed _____ w.p.m.

Special talents _____

Personal references:	Name	Address	Position	Phone

Previous experience: Employer	Address	Nature of work	Length of service from year to year

In what areas do you feel particularly strong? _____

In what areas do you feel particularly limited? _____

Why do you think you would like to be a teacher aide? _____

_____   _____
Date   Applicant's signature

questions such as: What would you do if_____? How do you feel about_____? Why do you think_____? You may be asked to join with other aide applicants in a group discussion on some topic having to do with the aide's role, or you may be asked to take part in a role-playing situation. The reason for this screening is to give interviewers some idea of how you would react in various situations. Usually the interviewer is looking for specific desirable characteristics. For example, the following items will probably be considered:

1. An aide should be physically able to carry out assigned duties and to be on the job regularly.
2. The aide should be emotionally stable and able to use good judgment in working with children and adults.
3. The aide should be able to speak well and to communicate effectively with the children and have the voice quality that does not detract from communication.
4. The aide should have the appearance and manners which will fit into the classroom environment and not detract from its effectiveness.
5. The aide should have the educational background that is necessary to help the students.
6. The aide should be open to suggestions for improvement and willing to put effort and time into developing skills.
7. The aide should have the ability to play a positive role with the children, encouraging them in their work, and being understanding of them in their problems.

Some districts offer prospective aides an opportunity to go into the classroom to observe and, in some cases, work for a day or two in order to have a better understanding of their role. Such an opportunity also enables the teacher to see the prospective aide in the working environment. This is helpful to both parties.

When you are hired and assigned, your questions about your role will be many and varied. This is natural, and you should feel free to ask questions and to receive answers. Some schools have written a handbook for aides; if so, it may include all the information you need to start. If your school does not have such a handbook, here are some questions you may want answers to:

1. What is your chain of command?
2. What procedures are set up for checking in and out?
3. What are the lunchroom policies?
4. What are the playground rules?

5. What first aid measures will you be expected to take?
6. Who in the school is the audiovisual expert?
7. What housekeeping duties are not in your domain?
8. How are supplies acquired for the classroom?
9. How are library materials and other instructional media acquired?
10. What procedure should you follow if you are late? Absent?
11. What is the daily schedule—bells, class schedule, recess, bus, lunch?
12. What is the fire-drill procedure?
13. What forms are required for you to use, and how should they be used?

Your supervising teacher will be able to answer most of these questions for you.

Before you enter the classroom, it will be helpful for you to think about three points in relation to your job as an aide. Why are aides needed? What are some of the things which are not in your area of responsibilities? What are some of the things you may be assigned to do?

why aides are needed The teacher needs an aide because the changing methods in teaching make more demands on teachers. This is very true, but let us focus a little more sharply on the things which are possible when there is an aide in the room.

A teacher is able to carry out a complete lesson with a group of children without interruptions from other children. This is important. It is distracting to both the teacher and the group involved in an important learning situation when, just as the climax is reached, a child from out of the group comes up for help. The point the teacher was making may be lost and it may be difficult for the teacher to get the children's attention again. With an aide in the classroom, the individual child can come to the aide for help when the teacher is in the middle of a lesson. The aide will not necessarily be able to handle each situation, but the chances of helping children on an individual basis increase with two adults in the room.

The grouping flexibility increases with an aide in the classroom. The teacher is able to tutor or counsel one student while the aide is available to help the others, or the teacher and the aide may conduct small group meetings, leaving a few children to work independently.

Discipline problems are also taken care of more quickly and more efficiently when the teacher is able to move with the troubled student away from the class, feeling confident that the class will still remain in control under the aide's guidance.

The teacher can be free from many nonprofessional tasks that normally require as much as one-third of the teaching time; thus the teacher can spend more time teaching.

The teacher is able to introduce more concepts to children because he or she does not need to stay with the group while lessons are reinforced either by drills, individual activities, or group projects, many of which the aide is able to conduct. Thus, the teacher can move on to the next group.

tasks for which an aide is not responsible You should know what tasks are not normally in the aide's realm of duty. Some of these are:

1. Organization of curriculum.
2. Evaluation of the students.
3. Deciding on educational materials and methods to be used.
4. Subjective entries in pupil records.
5. Developing evaluative instruments.
6. Conferring with parents.
7. Referring students for special help or assignments.
8. Making lesson plans.
9. Deciding on discipline methods.
10. Setting classroom policy.
11. Counseling students in their educational plans.

These duties require specialized knowledge of the teacher. When you begin a new job, you may go over this list with your supervising teacher and ask if there are other duties to be added to the list.

tasks for which an aide is responsible The duties which you as a teacher's aide will have depend on the policy of the school system and on the way individual teachers wish to work within the school system's policy. Your duties may include both those tasks which are not and those which are related to teaching.

clerical tasks Your clerical tasks may include telephone duties, filing, typing, ordering, and keeping records. The following list explains some of the clerical duties you might have:

1. Besides answering the telephone, you may have to contact parents to set up parent-teacher conferences, to inquire about a child who has been absent from school, and to discuss other routine matters which the teacher does not have to handle personally.

Aides may help with many of the clerical duties, such as typing and filing.

An aide is using a copy machine (another method of duplicating materials for classroom use).

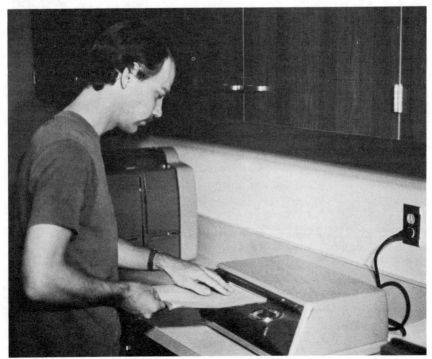

2. Set up and maintain a filing system of all correspondence, reports, tests, and instructional materials.
3. Type and duplicate business letters, papers, forms, weekly schedules, and report cards.
4. Order supplies, free instructional materials, and magazines for school or classroom use, and if necessary pick up and deliver ordered material. Keep inventory of all supplies and equipment as they come in and as they are used in the classroom.
5. Check and keep a record of daily attendance. Organize and maintain seating charts. Keep records of class schedules and maintain student records and child progress reports.

An aide is duplicating material which will later be used in the classroom.

housekeeping tasks You will probably be expected to help the teacher maintain a clean, orderly, and attractive classroom. The following lists some of the duties which may be your responsibility:

1. Everyday housekeeping tasks include sharpening pencils, cleaning chalkboards, covering books, cleaning spills, watering plants, and feeding fish.
2. Help the teacher before art lessons to assemble the material necessary

The aide may be in charge of maintaining supplies. This may include ordering supplies, keeping inventory of available supplies, and stocking the supply shelf when new material comes in.

for the lesson—easels, paints, clay. Make sure paste jars are full and paper cut as necessary. After the art lesson, you may have to supervise as the children clean up.

3. Help set up and disassemble science experiments.

4. Decorate bulletin boards and classrooms either with children's work or with other displays. You will have to learn how to cut mats for pictures and mount pictures. Make sure all bulletin boards and learning centers are kept up to date.

5. Take charge of audiovisual materials. This task may involve making sure that the equipment will be available when necessary, setting it up and operating it, and returning it when it is no longer needed.

other non-instruction-related tasks   Besides clerical and general housekeeping tasks, there are other duties which are not related to teaching.   You may have to relieve the teacher of at least some of these responsibilities.

1. Supervise loading and unloading of school buses.
2. Supervise children in the cafeteria.
3. Monitor study halls.
4. Take children to the nurse's office. If necessary, give first aid. Help with health record tasks, such as weighing, measuring heights, and testing eyes.

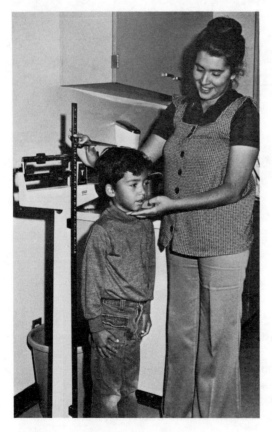

One of an aide's tasks may be to help the school nurse weigh and measure children.

5. Take children to the library.
6. Prepare and serve snacks.
7. Supervise after school activities, such as club meetings and classroom newspapers.
8. Help take children on field trips.

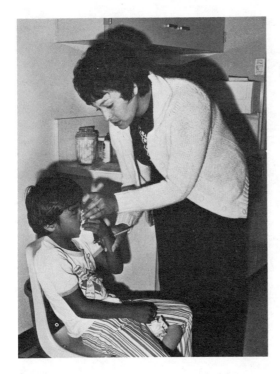

The aide helps the school nurse care for a sick child.

instruction-related tasks Although it will not be your responsibility to teach children, many of your duties may be closely related to teaching. If you are part of a team teaching group, you will be expected to attend team meetings and in-service training sessions.

When the teacher must leave the room temporarily, you will have to take charge of the classroom.

You may have to help gather material for use in the classroom. You may be involved in the following tasks:

1. Make flash cards.
2. Find library materials to be used by the children or by the teacher.
3. Prepare and organize resource materials for future use, such as picture files, audiovisual aids, and tapes.
4. Manage a classroom library or a resource center.

At times you may have to work very closely with the children. The following are some duties which the teacher may assign to you:

1. Help children find source materials for independent activities, special reports, and small group projects.

The teacher aide may have a variety of instruction-related
tasks. Here the aide is helping a child take part in a touch
discriminatory experience.

2. Supervise study groups.
3. Assist in a variety of reading functions. Conduct story hours in the
   lower grades. Help slow readers and listen to children read aloud.
4. Repeat lessons to slow learners or to children who have been absent.
5. Help conduct drills and supervise seatwork. For example, you may
   have to conduct arithmetic drills and read vocabulary and spelling lists.

You may be asked to assist the teacher during lessons:

1. Besides supervising unstructured playground activities, you may have to
   teach and supervise games and help organize intramural athletic programs.
2. Supervise some physical education activities.
3. Assist in teaching dance.

The teacher aide may be asked to give individual help to
new students or to students who have been absent for a few
days.

4. Help with the chorus, or accompany music classes with a piano or auto-harp.
5. Assist teacher during craft lessons.
6. Supervise when children are doing science experiments.
7. Help teach children tool safety.
8. Proctor examinations.
9. Use answer keys provided by the teacher to correct workbooks, seatwork, and tests.

The Aide and the Child

The emphasis here is on *working with the child.* Knowing
curriculum is important. Working with the system and with adults is
important. However, it is with the child that the most important

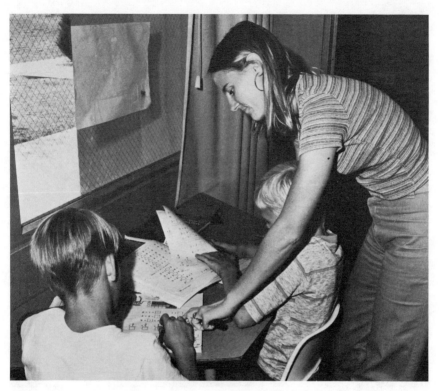

The teacher aide may be asked to help children with seatwork. This aide is helping children with their arithmetic
workbooks.

work is to be achieved. Children are different in some ways, and
these differences must be understood. Children are also similar in
some ways, and these similarities can sometimes provide us with
guidelines on how to deal with them.

The first thing to remember about all children is that they are
human beings who have been born recently and are living in a world
filled with a tremendous variety of things. They have needs which
go beyond the physical and material. These needs are love, understanding, acceptance, goals, encouragement, respect, responsibilities, and limits. Sometimes it is very hard to recognize a child's
need, and to find an effective way of helping to satisfy it. Children
want you to understand them but are not always willing to disclose
their feelings; so you may become confused when you deal with
them. Dr. Haim G. Ginott, in his book *Between Parent and Child,*
provides a guide for interpreting the child's real needs and suggests
how to deal with these needs.

This teacher is free to work with a small group of children
on a special project while the teacher's aide is showing a
film to the rest of the class.

Sometimes children need help in recognizing their problems.
It is important for children to know that an adult can understand
their problems and can accept that their problems are real. Take for
instance a child who comes back from recess thoroughly discouraged
and on the verge of tears. Through some detective work you may
discover that this child, who was the last one chosen for the baseball
team, came up to bat and struck out. To remind the child of his or
her high academic standing is not going to be very comforting. Let
the child know that you realize the situation must have been em-
barassing and that it is natural to feel dejection and anger when one
has an opportunity to prove oneself and fails. When you accept
these feelings with understanding and empathy, the intensity of the
hurt is lessened.

As Dr. Haim Ginott points out in *Between Parent and Child,*
when talking to children it is important for the teacher and aide to remember that children, as adults, are able to feel two ways about a
person.[3] You can like and dislike a person at the same time. This is
difficult for some people to accept. People have a tendency to want
it either/or—either I like you or I don't. Not only are these mixed

[3] Ginott, Haim, G. *Between Parent and Child.* New York: The Macmillan Co., 1965,
p. 33.

feelings frustrating to both children and adults, but many people are not able to deal with negative feelings comfortably. They have been taught that it is wrong to dislike people, to feel angry, to be frightened. So they tend to hide these feelings, and feel guilty because of them. Children do the same thing and are burdened with guilt. If you can let the child know that it is all right to have these mixed and negative feelings, then the burden may be lessened.

One of the easiest ways to work positively with children is to praise them. It is easy to pat a child on the head and say: You sure are a good kid, or You sure are smart. Sometimes after you make such a statement the child may react negatively. You should try to understand the child's feelings. At some time or another you have undoubtedly received praise knowing it wasn't fully justified. The act for which you were praised may have required little effort, your motives may have been selfish or you may have felt that the job was not well done. Therefore you may have felt embarrassed by the praise, disappointed because you felt you should have done more, frightened that you might be found out, and suspicious of the person who made the complimentary comments. In the same way, a child may react negatively to unfounded or insincere praise. The resulting feelings are difficult for the child to deal with. As Dr. Ginott points out, when you praise a child, your praise should be descriptive. It should deal with the child's efforts and accomplishments, not with the child's character and personality.[4] For instance, if a child hands in a paper that is better than usual, the child should be told that it is neat, thorough, well researched, or whatever. Having put forth more effort to make it better, the child will be pleased to accept your compliment because it is realistic and well deserved.

It is important to know not only how to give praise, but also how to give constructive criticism. If a paper is handed in that is below the expected standard, the teacher may be tempted to tear the paper up in front of the class, show it to the group as a bad example, or scold the individual for being sloppy. However, a more helpful, positive attitude would be to assume that the child will want to do the paper over and to offer some directions to help the student get started on it.

It is important to remember that children are just learning to live in the world. In order to learn what works and what doesn't, what one feels good about and what one doesn't, what others will accept and what they won't, one has to experiment and try things.

[4] Ibid.

Sometimes children may lie when trying to cope with some situations. Adults have such strong feelings against lying that it is sometimes difficult to deal with such trial behavior in a way that will be helpful to the child.

Very often adults put children in a position where they almost have to rely on lying to get them out of a difficult situation. For instance, when you find a book which the child has marked up and glare at the child in almost open anger and demand, Did you write in this book? This young person is being pushed into lying and saying, No, because he or she is too frightened to admit it. After some time, children come to know that when people approach them in that manner the next step can be pretty painful. This is not to say that the whole situation should be ignored. The child should be made aware of what he or she has done. A possible way of dealing with such situations would be to ask the child a series of questions. You might start the questions by asking, What did you do? Do not accept silence or I don't know as an answer. The child must verbalize what he or she did. Your other questions might be, Did it help you? Did it help anyone else? Is there something else you could do? Is there some other way of handling this situation, something else you could say, etc.? This gives the child an opportunity to take care of the problem positively if it should happen again. If you use this routine, you should ask the questions without emotion or preaching so the child can truly concentrate on answering the questions and not fear your reaction. Often the adult will write the child's answers on a card, complete with suggestions of how he or she plans to deal with the situation next time. Then, if the same thing does happen again, they can both go back and see that either the child didn't follow the plan, or that it didn't work, and that the child is going to have to think up a new way of dealing with this problem.

It is not unusual for children to take things which do not belong to them. If you know the child has taken something, make sure you don't play games in your questioning. Don't ask if the child did take something or if the child knows who took it. Instead, calmly state, The pencil you have belongs to Tim, or The money that you put in your pocket is Janet's lunch money. Then be sure to stay with the situation until the object is returned to its rightful owner.

Very often in modern education we talk about allowing children to make choices. It must be realized that making choices is a responsibility, and one which children have to be helped to attain. Children are not helped but rather are hurt if they are put in a position of making a choice they are not ready to make, and the results are a discouraging failure for them. In most situations, children will not be given the choice whether or not they are going to study math this year, but may be given the choice of which sequence of math sections they will study, what part of the day they are going to work on it, what activities they will use to learn it. At first, children may have the choice only of what experiences they will involve themselves in; later, they add to it until very often the children gain enough knowledge about themselves and their needs so that they can schedule their whole week with very little guidance from the classroom's adults. Making choices also carries over in the ways of working and living with other people. Children can often tell when a very difficult situation is facing them. They realize that if they stay in the environment that they are in, they are going to react to the situation in some unacceptable manner. If they know this, they should be encouraged to take what steps they need to help them over this period. They may be allowed and even encouraged to go outside and take a walk around the playground, come to an adult and tell of their problem, or talk with a special friend, and then rejoin the group when the tension is over. Although you should be very cautious in allowing children to make too many choices, you should also be sure to allow them to make choices where they are comfortably able to do so. When children live in a situation where they are smothered by other people making their decisions, they are not interested in setting goals for themselves; they lack the know-how of getting things done on their own, and they never enjoy the satisfaction of a job well done.

People who work with children want to be liked by them. When a small child comes up and takes you by the hand and says I love you, it is sheer ecstasy. However, you should not need the child's acceptance so much that you would do anything for it. Otherwise, the child will be able to manipulate you. There will be times when you will make demands and decisions which are not popular. You will have to uphold rules which the children feel to be unfair. You will have to set limits which are considered too strict. You might let the children know that you realize they don't agree with your decisions and that you know they are angry, but that you have given it serious thought and this, in your opinion, is the best way to handle the situation. You might also let them know that this is the situation for the present time. Indicate that perhaps the situation may change and you will be willing to reconsider any new ideas that come along.

It is important that children know acceptable and unacceptable behavior. In a school situation, limits are set by parents, school administration, the principal and staff at the school, the teacher, the student council, the aide, or the child, and most times by a combination of these. It is necessary that children be acquainted with the limits and that they respect them. A child becomes frustrated when prohibited behavior is accepted or ignored. Very often the child interprets this as a lack of concern on the part of the tolerating adult.

We spoke earlier of the differences in children. Differences in physical make up, mental abilities, emotional patterns, social and economic backgrounds have been given attention for a long time, and most of us are aware of these and have in some way learned to deal with them. We may need to take a close look at the ways in which we do so. Do we automatically expect more from a Caucasian child than from a child of another race? Research studies show that a child's aptitude does not depend on race, but many adults in the school systems do expect more of Caucasian children. This attitude of the adults has affected the learning of the minority race children.

Children are different. These children are of the same age but vary in physical development.

Do we automatically expect the same talents, aptitudes, and values from sisters and brothers? Most of the time we are very surprised when we find that one member of a family does not fit into the same pattern of another sibling. Do we usually expect children with emotional problems to be less intelligent than the normal child, although realizing that many of our real geniuses had emotional problems? These differences need to be studied and dealt with on an individual basis. Try to find out what your real thinking is on these attitudes. Where do you *really* stand, how will you *really* react, what will you *really* do when your task is to work with these differences?

Another difference that adults need to be aware of is that children came into this world such a short time ago. They were not here when the very important things that help shape *our* attitudes and values happened. They were not affected by them and they cannot relate to them as we do. Their world is different from ours. We are shocked by their apparent lack of respect. They have respect—although it may differ from ours—for many people and many situations. We are concerned because they don't appreciate the material things, and yet these things have always been a part of their lives and have always been easily accessible to them. In some ways, their lives are much broader than ours were at their age. They have traveled more; they have lived in more places; television has introduced them to the world and all its people and situations. Their pace of living is fast, with many experiences packed into each day. But in some ways their lives are much more narrow than those of people in the past. In many instances they come from small families—one- or two-children homes without grandparents. They do not have the experience of living with many members of a family, such as in an extended family. Their social life in elementary school years is usually limited to children of friends of their parents. These people have similar living situations, backgrounds, and values. These are just a few of the differences between you and the children you are dealing with. It is important to try to understand the child's world instead of always trying to make the child understand your world.

We have mentioned the term *individual differences* several times. We can't talk about human relationships without considering individual differences. Although you may know that all individuals are different, it may be hard to understand the real meaning of the term. We tend to reason that if children are born of the same parents and raised in the same environment, they should be carbon copies of the older children in the family, but it does not happen that way. We tend to think that all children should be walking by the time they are one year old, talking by eighteen months, reading by seven years, and ready for all adult responsibilities by the age of eighteen, but it does not happen that way either. People grow at different rates, and when we say *grow* we are talking about more than height or weight. People grow in four different ways: physically, mentally, emotionally, and socially. Growth is influenced by parentage, environment, culture, etc. When we stop to think about the many factors which contribute to the shaping of a single human being, it becomes frightening to think about the responsibilities of a person who is working with young children. Fortunately, there are some reliable growth norms, and if we don't lean too heavily on them, they can be a good guide when we work with children. The important thing is for educators to accept the differences they find in children who may be the same age but who are all at various stages of growth, and to be alert to any problems these differences may present.

Teachers, teacher aides, and all people who deal with school children should be aware that each child will react to the school environment in a different way. Most children look forward to starting school and very often enjoy it. However, each child enjoys different aspects of school and has different objectives.

Some children enjoy the whole school setup. Even when they are at home, they play school with their friends. They find the school routine comfortable and try to conform to the image of the good pupil. They are anxious to read and do well in school.

Other children enjoy those aspects of school which encourage them not to conform. They love to play and enjoy having so many other children in the classroom to play with. However, they are not interested in much of the structured program in the school. They do not like to sit quietly while reading or writing or to listen to instructions. They enjoy active games where they can run and yell.

Because of these differences some children will progress very rapidly in the primary grades. As the children become older, many of these differences become less important. The children who progressed slowly at first eventually catch up with their classmates.

Children also differ in their physical development. Girls mature more rapidly and earlier than boys. Girls are first to enter the period before puberty. This period is marked by changes in body proportions, metabolism, and balance of body hormones. At this time, the girls become interested in boys (usually in the fourth or fifth grades). They will try to get the boys' attention in many ways. The boys who have not reached the same age of development will chase and fight with the girls but usually prefer other boys as play-

mates. Eventually the boys go through puberty and also become
interested in girls. These stages of development on the way to
maturity are often difficult for both sexes.

Educators have a special regard for primary teachers—especially kindergarten teachers who are often called blessed, super-
human, unbelievable. Teachers of older students have a hard time
figuring out how any teacher can take thirty human beings who have
only lived five years and turn out thirty students who are able to conform to the school environment and have gained some academic
skills. There are some aspects of the four-and five-year olds' growth
patterns that help this change take place; other aspects often hinder
desirable changes.

The age of four is active. The four-year-olds run, race, talk,
roll, jump, and ask questions constantly. They ask questions more
often just to be doing something rather than to gain information, as
they seldom wait for an answer before asking another question.
They talk with anyone who will listen and often engage strangers in

Children at ages four to five enjoy make believe. These children are playing in the housekeeping corner of the kindergarten.

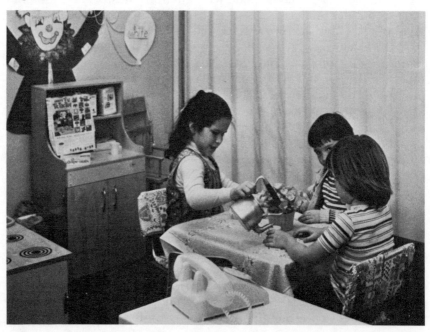

conversation. They enjoy dramatic play and have wonderful imaginations. Make-believe is very real to them, and this is a suitable time to teach them things through role playing. Their ability to make up stories is great at this age because they do not understand limits or constraints. A special joy for them is to tell a story and have it recorded so they can listen to it again and again. The large muscles in their bodies are developing so they can do a lot of climbing, go up stairs using alternate feet, and throw at a target (which they seldom even come close to). Physical play that involves jumping, climbing, or running is excellent large-muscle activity for four-year-olds. They are not quite ready for skipping, hopping, and other play calling for balance. Large blocks, bean bags, clay, finger paints, crayons, pail and shovel work, and any other activity calling for fine neuromuscular coordination are their favorites.

At five children become less explosive and quite mature. They tend to be less open than the four-year-olds. They are shy around strangers. They want to do those things which are familiar to them and rebel against new experiences. They want old possessions around them, and find security in following a routine or in following an example. Very often if one child in the class does something or says something, all the other children in the class will do or say the same thing. They can sit for longer periods of time and listen now, so they enjoy story telling and quiet games. They may play with clay and paint for long periods of time. Their active play shows comparatively good large-muscle control. They can balance themselves more easily, kick a ball farther, and can hop, skip, and march to music. They throw a ball with fair accuracy now. They like to get involved in games with older children, such as baseball, jump-rope, hopscotch, etc. They are beginning to play with groups of children but usually do not play for long without some friction. They do best when playing with only one friend. It is important that an adult working with children of this age make it very plain to them what is expected of them, as their nature is to be cooperative and to follow rules. If they break a rule, it is usually unknowingly and they feel very sorry about it.

At six, our model students turn into public enemies. They talk all the time, get into everything, and move constantly. It seems that at this time of life, they are never at their best. They want everything their own way and often pout and cry if they cannot have their way. They go from one extreme to another. At one moment they love the world and everyone in it, and the next moment they are mad at the world and can't stand their own best friend. This is an age of experimentation for children. They are willing to try almost everything: their limits, strengths, and other people's patience. Whatever they do, they do it enthusiastically and actively. In fact, they are in constant motion and need to be watched so that they do not overdo. Most six-year-olds are fairly well advanced in manual dexterity and hand-and-foot coordination. They skip well and climb well, and they can kick a small object with ease. They can bounce a ball for a fair length of time, but they are not too concerned about how well they do it or in improving their skill.

It is important to note that while their hand-and-foot coordination is fairly well developed, eye-hand coordination is still in a comparatively early development stage. Six-year-olds are generally frustrated when they attempt to play with anything which calls for greater finger dexterity and space judgment. Therefore, it is advisable that in ball games, a ball the size of a volleyball or even a bean bag be used. Eye-hand coordination is important in reading and writing skills. The child will have a difficult time learning to read or write until eye-hand coordination improves. It is very important that children not be pressured or criticized about learning skills until they are able to learn them. It is better to provide children with activities that will help develop their eye-hand coordination and postpone typical reading instruction until they are ready for it. Pushing too hard now, before children are really able to succeed, very often turns them against reading. As a result, the child may have reading problems throughout school and perhaps for life.

Six-year-olds need lots of careful guidance and protection to shelter them from constant frustration. They want to be sociable and are trying to learn social skills. Until now they have only been concerned with themselves and cannot learn social skills immediately. They want to become independent, but the only way they know how to express their independence is to be aggressive and revolt against home, family, and other people. It seems that whatever they do is wrong, and they move from one scolding to another when what they really need is encouragement, praise, and guidance. Life is never dull around a six-year-old.

Thankfully, the six-year-old terrors become seven-year-old children who are more accepting of themselves and others. They understand rules and limits now and accept them. They enjoy being with others and are willing to listen and even ask for advice. They are becoming more interested in small-muscle activities. They enjoy shooting marbles, playing checkers, playing jacks, weaving, sewing, macramé, and other craft work. They also enjoy structured games and rough-and-tumble activities.

Eight-year-olds show very rapid physical and social growth. They are collectors, explorers, and adventurers. At this age, too, they love belonging to clubs. The more structured and more secret, the better it suits them. They still love rough-and-tumble games and arguing and exchanging criticism with their peers. However, they resent any criticism from adults. They are learning that they must respect authority, but they aren't liking it.

Many eight-year-olds have matured sufficiently to understand the concepts of teamwork and cooperation. Because of this, good social habits and democratic ideas can be formed now. Most eight-year-olds are very sociable. They have a difficult time entertaining themselves, as they always want to be with a group. They love rewards, so points, stars, money, or almost anything else is a great motivator for them.

Eight-year-olds have good coordination. Their balance is good, and they coordinate their hands and legs well. They are beginning to acquire side vision. They are learning to divide their attention so they can take directions and put them into practice at the same time. They are becoming quite graceful. This physical growth coupled with their actual social growth makes them eager team participants.

From age nine through elementary school, children continue to grow and develop their physical, emotional, mental, and social skills. They are much more concerned about their skills and work to improve them. They are tough critics of their own ability. They may shoot baskets for hours, practice their music scales over and over, and knit and ravel their stitches until they feel they have done it right.

During this period, the child has reached the age of great loyalty to the social group. The child's concern for his or her own family has gained in importance, but loyalty to the gang is placed above all else. Children form clubs and break up clubs just as rapidly. They are usually very loyal to their clubs and do not accept criticism well.

Children enjoy team activities such as team sports, spelling bees, and math races. Children also enjoy games or activities where one individual from a group competes with another individual from another group.

Although many children of this age group are well coordinated, others are still pudgy and do not have well-developed neuromuscular skills. Often these children are the last to be chosen when teams are picked. You should watch so that these children are not left out of games. They will reach their peers' level of coordination eventually. In the meantime they should not be allowed to feel inferior to the other children.

Children of this age have very deep feelings of right and wrong, and for them things are either right or wrong; there is no in-between. They also tend to feel what is fair for one is fair for all, and for them there is not much room for individual differences. Also their peer image is very important to them and must be protected and understood by those working with them. You should not try to change their minds, argue with them, or threaten them in front of their peers. When a problem comes up, you should get them away from the others and then you will be able to have a very reasonable talk. They are willing to listen then and may even be of help to the adult in influencing the others in the group.

Children of this age particularly dislike being interrupted in what they are doing, be it on the playground or in the classroom. Because of this their routine should be well organized and set for them. If there are going to be changes in the classroom or playground routine, the children should be informed before they have time to get involved in an activity. It is well to go over a daily schedule with the children before the day starts and explain any change in the schedule at that time. If certain students are going to be involved in some special work or activities, it is wise to inform them of any change in plans as soon as possible so they can prepare for it.

The preceding pages have given you a look at some of the situations which come up when you deal with children, of some ways to handle them, and some things you need to think about when you begin working with children for several hours each day. The view has been a very small one. It was not meant to satisfy all your concerns, but to make you aware of conditions and situations you had not thought about before. More questions and concerns will come to you, and you will feel compelled to search out more positive ways of working with children. Many articles have been written to help in dealing with children. Some of them provide background; some of them give ideas; some of them are meant to excite you and help you become more inspired in your job. Search out these materials. Look in libraries, bookstores, magazine stands; ask teachers and other educators for suggestions; attend workshops and classes. If you can work with the child in a positive manner, the rest of the job usually takes care of itself.

Aides and Teachers

Teachers are as different as aides and students. Their individuality should be appreciated. A variety of teachers and methods are effective with the many different types of children. Teachers set the tone of the classroom. Some teachers work best in a well-organized, structured environment, where previously made plans are followed carefully. At the other end of the range is the more informal teacher. Plans are made by this teacher as the day progresses, and the room atmosphere is open and free. Both types may be exceptionally competent teachers. Both types can work well with some children and not be very successful with others. This is also true in their relationship with aides. Not all aides match up perfectly with all teachers. In some cases, a difference works out well. The aide may supply needed organizational skill or project a warmth toward children that the teacher is unable to give. As a result everyone benefits. If these personal differences present a problem, a change should be requested, as children sense difficulties and the effectiveness of the team will be lost. However, in most cases, as the teacher sees the

The teacher and aide may work together designing bulletin boards and discussing class assignments.

aide sharing the concerns, the problems, and the enjoyment, the team spirit and effectiveness will grow.

In team teaching, remember that even if the team is made up of only you and your teacher, it is a team. It is important that you understand how your teacher and the school see discipline and what methods and techniques are used in helping children learn acceptable behavior. Find out as soon as possible what the rules of the classroom are, and then help enforce them in a positive manner. Ask what kinds of behavior situations the teacher wants to take care of personally, which are reported to the office, whether you should report any problems, and which problems you should handle alone.

As in any family relationship, there are times when two people do not agree as to what action should be taken in handling a discipline problem. It is very important that you uphold and support the action that the teacher has taken. Never question the action in front of the children, and of course do not say anything to the children to make them think you don't agree. Children need to feel the unity of the team. If you feel the treatment was wrong, talk with your teacher about it alone. There may be some circumstances influencing the teacher's actions of which you are not aware, or the teacher, being human, has acted before thinking the whole thing through carefully.

The kind of aide that every teacher hopes for has some very special qualities. Perhaps one of the most frequently desired is enthusiasm for the job. In working together, the teacher knows the aide enjoys working with the children and likes being with the adults in the classroom situation. The aide transmits the excitement experienced in watching the progress that the children make, and responds positively to the way a professional builds a learning environment. The aide adjusts to changes whether in daily plans or the moods of the people, and realizes that all jobs have their pleasant parts and the not-so-pleasant parts, and takes a fair share of both. The aide is able to see things that need to be done and does not stand around waiting to be told by the teacher what to do next. However, at the same time, the aide realizes that the teacher is the leader in the classroom, and does not overstep the bounds of the role separating aide and teacher. The relationship of aide to children is understood and enjoyed. It is not a role of mother, sister, or buddy. The role is to help the teacher and the children. The aide should work constantly to improve in the position by taking part in workshops, enrolling in aide classes, reading pertinent materials, and asking for help and advice. Finally, the aide achieves personal fulfillment in knowing the children are helped in their learning through the aide's efforts.

Evaluation

The teacher's aide like all other school personnel takes part in an evaluation procedure. This is an opportunity for the evaluator to talk over the job assignment with the aide, clearing up any misconceptions, and giving valuable information and suggestions.

The evaluation usually consists of a written evaluation form and a discussion. The primary responsibility for evaluation of the aide usually rests with the school administrator (principal), but in a team situation the aide's teacher is given an opportunity to see the formal evaluation form and react to it. Many times the teacher and the principal work together to complete the form and determine the topics which will be covered in the discussion. The evaluation should be a positive way to help the aide become better and more effective.

The evaluation procedure is usually determined in the district. It is used primarily by the teacher or principal in evaluating the aide, but it may also be used effectively by the aide in self-evaluation. It also serves the purpose of making both the teacher and the aide aware of what is desired of the aide.

Two sample evaluation forms are included here. The first, entitled "Teacher Aide Rating Scale Form" shown on page 40 is an example of an evaluation form which might be used by a principal, teacher, or personnel officer. It is short and objective. However, each point accompanied with comments and suggestions can be effective. The second example is the "Teacher Aide Evaluation Form" shown on pages 41–42. This evaluation form expands on the same topics. It is more valuable for the aide as a means of self-evaluation. It is in itself an in-service teaching device for teacher aides. Study both evaluation forms to see what points are considered in an evaluation.

Remember that the evaluation procedure is or should be *a positive learning experience for you*. Ask your evaluator to explain points that you are not sure about. Ask for suggestions on how you can improve. Accept these suggestions in a positive way, and do not feel that you are being attacked. This is a time set aside for the team to think only about you and ways they can help you. Make the most of it!

TEACHER AIDE RATING SCALE FORM

_____ School District

Teacher aide name / Supervising teacher / Date

	Out-standing	Above average	Average	Below average	Unsatis-factory
1 Personal appearance and grooming					
2. Courtesy					
3. Attitude					
4. Resourcefulness					
5. Reliability					
6. Initiative					
7. Cooperation					
8. Competence					
9. Efficiency					
10. Punctuality and attendance					
11. Flexibility					
12. Communication skills					

Additional comments and observations _____

_____
_____
_____
_____
_____

TEACHER AIDE EVALUATION FORM

_____ School District

SCALE	
5	exceptional
4	above average
3	average
2	below average
1	unsatisfactory

Date _____

Grade level _____

Name _____

Supervising
Teacher _____

__ 1. Shows empathy in working with students and their problems.

__ 2. Can be depended on to carry out assigned tasks.

__ 3. Demonstrates reliability in assigned responsibilities.

__ 4. Is able to change to meet new and different situations.

__ 5. Is helpful whenever possible.

__ 6. Is courteous at all times, even when provoked.

__ 7. Is competent in subject matter areas.

__ 8. Is cheerful and pleasant and exhibits a positive attitude.

__ 9. Gathers materials to be used in the classroom.

__10. Arrives at school on time.

__11. Is on the job most of the time and has legitimate reasons when not.

__12. Exhibits good personal care and grooming.

__13. Is in good physical health.

__14. Shows ability to master new techniques.

__15. Is alert and aware of what is going on.

__16. Is friendly with staff and students.

__17. Keeps classroom neat and orderly.

__18. Performs clerical work efficiently.

__19. Is able to operate audiovisual and other teaching devices.

__20. Follows directions.

__21. Works well without direct supervision.

__22. Is fair in dealing with students.

__23. Provides a pleasant learning atmosphere.

__24. Is able to motivate students to want to learn.

__25. Uses good grammar.

__26. Encourages freedom of oral exchange with the student.

__27. Remains calm and collected when emergencies arise.

__28. Uses time wisely.

__29. Uses instructional materials efficiently without waste.

__30. Exhibits patience with and understanding of annoying and disruptive behavior.

__31. Uses discretion in discussing school matters.

__32. Speaks positively about the school, school district, and community.

__33. Is aware of and follows school rules and policies.

__34. Prepares for assigned tasks.

__35. Is energetic and shows enthusiasm in learning activities.

__36. Shows good voice control.

__37. Is willing to seek information needed.

__38. Accepts criticism and suggestions well.

__39. Shows respect for the rights, feelings, and opinions of others.

__40. Likes children and wants to help them.

__41. Understands the differences in the roles of the teacher and the teacher aide.

__42. Understands children who have problems.

__43. Enjoys the work of a teacher aide.

__44. Has gained the respect and admiration of the students.

__45. Has shown growth and progress during the school year.

Chapter Summary

The demand for teacher aides in the classroom has rapidly increased in recent years and indications are that they will be used even more in years to come.

Teacher aides are used in many and varied ways. Generally, they are used to do the things that need to be done but can be done by someone with less professional training than a teacher.

Since the vocation of teacher aide is relatively new, the job description and educational prerequisites have not been agreed upon by all educators. It is, however, agreed by many that it is highly desirable for aides to have in addition to a high school education at least some specialized training. Many post-high school educational institutions offer one- and two-year curriculums in the training of teacher aides.

Aides come from many backgrounds and vary in age, sex, creed, race, and other ways. They should all have a common desire to help children learn. The aide should be eager to learn about all the phases of the job in order to increase classroom effectiveness. Aides will need to know the school, its organization, personnel, facilities, and equipment and resource materials available. They must learn to work as part of the instructional team. They will have to learn what things are their responsibility and what are those of the teacher.

Teacher aides should put great emphasis on understanding children. They need to understand that children are different in many ways and alike in many ways, and that these differences and similarities need to be studied seriously. They should remember that children have limited knowledge and experience, and that children's needs exceed physical and material needs. These needs include such things as love, understanding, encouragement, respect, responsibility, and the knowledge of limits.

Teacher aides must have a great deal of patience and perseverance in order to learn what is necessary to be proficient in their job. Evaluations can be extremely useful in helping aides to develop and use their strengths effectively, and to recognize and improve their weaker points.

Suggested References

Anderson, Robert H. (ed.). *Education in Anticipation of Tomorrow.* Worthington, Ohio: Charles A. Jones Publishing Company, 1973.

Anderson, Robert H. *Teaching in a World of Change.* New York: Harcourt, Brace and World, Inc., 1966.

Ashton-Warner, Sylvia. *Teacher.* New York: Simon and Schuster, Inc., 1963.

Becker, Harry A. (ed.). "Working with Teacher Aides," *Croft Leadership Action Folio.* New London, Conn.: Croft Educational Services, 1968.

Brotherson and Johnson. *Teacher Aide Handbook.* Danville, Ill.: Interstate Printers and Publishers, Inc., 1971.

Featherstone, Joseph. *Schools Where Children Learn.* New York: Liveright Publisher Corporation, 1971.

Gentry, Robert J. "Why Teacher Aides?" *The Preparation of BIA Teacher and Dormitory Aides.* Vols. I, II, III. Prepared by Avco Economic Systems Corporation under the Elementary and Secondary Education Act for the Bureau of Indian Affairs, Department of Interior, 1967.

Gesell, Arnold, and Ilg, Frances L. *The Child from Five to Ten.* New York: Harper and Row Publishers, Incorporated, 1946.

Ginott, Haim G. *Between Parent and Child.* New York: The Macmillan Company, 1965.

————. *Between Parent and Teenager.* New York: The Macmillan Company, 1969.

————. *Teacher and Child.* New York: The Macmillan Company, 1972.

Glasser, William. *Schools without Failure.* New York: Harper and Row, Publishers, Incorporated, 1969.

Holt, John. *How Children Fail.* New York: Pitman Publishing Corporation, 1964.

————. *How Children Learn.* New York: Pitman Publishing Corporation, 1967.

————. *What Do I Do on Monday?* New York: E. P. Dutton and Co., Inc., 1970.

Howe, Robert. *The Teacher Assistant.* Dubuque, Iowa: Wm. C. Brown Company, 1972.

Kohl, Herbert R. *The Open Classroom.* New York: A New York Review Book, 1969.

Murrow, Casey, and Murrow, Liza. *Children Come First.* New York: American Heritage Press, 1971.

Neill, A. S. *Summerhill–A Radical Approach to Child Rearing.* New York: Hart Publishing Co., 1960.

Rathbone, Charles H. *Open Education: The Informal Classroom.* New York: Citation Press, 1971.

Shields, Gordon. *Instructional Associate.* Grossmont, California: Grossmont College in Cooperation with the California Community Colleges, 1972.

Introduction

Although teacher aides help teachers in all areas of the curriculum, they are of greatest help in the areas pertaining to communication. A common complaint among teachers is, If I could just get through a reading lesson without any interruptions the reading scores would soar. But every time I get to the climax of a story, I am interrupted by a child who needs help on work sheets or some such thing. By the time I can turn my attention back to the reading group, the continuity of the lesson and motivation are lost. The whole lesson is ruined. Another teacher may complain that although it is true that not all children learn how to spell by the same

method, as long as it is necessary to dictate a spelling list to some of the class, there is not enough time to give the others the type of attention they need. And teachers from kindergarten through college complain because they do not have enough time to correct written assignments and return them to the students fast enough. By the time the assignments are returned, they are no longer meaningful to the students. A properly trained aide can be of real value in helping resolve such problems.

Communication skills, also referred to as language arts skills, include any skills which involve communication between people. Stop and think what these might be. Of course, the main skill in

communication skills 2

communicating with others is speaking. But if you want to communicate by speaking, you must have a listener (someone with listening skills.) Another skill is writing. The skill that complements writing is reading. Thus the four major areas of communication are speaking, listening, writing, and reading. Each one is so important that it will be dealt with separately, but keep in mind that they are all component parts of that very important skill of communication.

Speaking

If you observe a classroom for just a few minutes, you will be tempted to remark that speaking is not a weak area. Much talking goes on in the classroom. In fact, to many observers, the problem may appear to be getting the children to stop talking. However, the problem is not to get them to stop, but to help them become better conversationalists. Perhaps the overall objective of the school could be to provide a well-organized program requiring the use of spoken language. Spoken, or oral, language should be as natural and spontaneous as possible. Nevertheless, it is necessary to plan for systematic practice of the skills which are needed for oral expression. Some techniques help make a person a better conversationalist. People who have various interests are fun to talk with. The partner in the conversation comes away from the discussion feeling that he or she has really added to his or her own growth by talking with such a person. A good conversationalist is also a good listener. Both partners must feel that the conversation was both an intake and an output of information. Not only are good conversationalists good listeners, but they are aware of clues from the conversational partner. The speaker reacts when the listener has something that he or she is really anxious to say, when the listener agrees with the speaker, when the listener is becoming bored by the discussion, and when the listener is ready to stop the conversation. The speaker should notice the clues and be willing to react to them. Perhaps voice quality, posture, articulation, and good grammar are also important, but many times these skills will come when the others are built. Poise and ease are the result of feeling adequate in a situation. The way to prepare children for ease in conversations in real life is to give them practice speaking at school. There are many different types of conversation situations, and as an aide you will be asked to direct some or help the teacher and children with others.

Discussion skills are very important, and many times opportunities to develop them are overlooked in the classroom because the teacher does not have enough time to prepare groups to take part in discussions. An aide in the classroom can do much in taking over some of the preparation. To prepare for discussion, resources must be available for the children. The more materials available, the more successful the discussion will probably be. Gather the classroom supplementary materials and raid the resource center of all the materials pertaining to the discussion topic. Another way to help would be to have the area set up where the discussion group is going to take place. If it is going to be a circle, have the chairs in a circle formation; if a table is needed, have one ready. It might be helpful to record the discussion for reviewing or evaluating purposes. If so, have the equipment set up. In some classes, pencil and paper may be needed. Have them ready. Preparation adds to the smoothness of the experience and makes it more meaningful.

One of the most common conversation situations is the small-group discussion. To provide practice in the small-group discussion, assign the child to a group that is discussing something that he or she is interested in. For instance, when studying about the colonial period, not every child is going to get really excited about the hardships the colonists endured. Perhaps some have very interesting ideas to contribute about how the Indians helped the settlers adapt to their new homes. Group the children according to their interest. The same idea works at book-report time. Book reports can be unbearable if every child has to sit and listen to every other child report on a book. However, interest soars and children look forward to reporting if all those who are interested in mysteries form a small group and report on their mystery books, if all sport-story lovers gather together to tell about the books on sports that they have read, and so on.

To help the small-group discussion be successful, use a seating arrangement where all the children sit facing each other. This is an important point, and if you need to, arrange seats in this way. Eye contact is important in conversations. Leaders are not necessary in small-group discussions.

How long should these conversations last? They should last as long as the children are bringing in fresh material, and when this is not happening, the activity should be stopped. You may find that some children have a very difficult time getting started on their contribution to the group even though it has been based on interests. Perhaps some format, agreed upon by the group, or some structure, developed by the class before the groups were made, would be helpful. For instance, in sharing a book with a group, the opening sentence may be simply: The title of my book is *The Hound of the Baskervilles* by Sir Arthur Conan Doyle. With this start, the child will be able to go on.

Small discussion groups are an effective way to begin building discussion skills. The children feel comfortable sharing information with friends in a small, easy, informal setting. In a small group, they can more readily check how their audience reacted to their report, which of their skills were successful and which needed more work. This gives the student practice in gaining poise and self-confidence.

But small-group discussions are not the only conversation situations you can use. Round-table discussions are useful from third grade through adult life. In this situation, a group leader is chosen or appointed. The subject to be discussed may be any problem in which the group is concerned. The situation is one in which to air opinions. The round-table discussion often deals with problems in which emotions are involved; therefore, a strong discussion leader is a must, and some strong guidelines need to be set down. If you are in charge of a round-table discussion, it would be wise for you to act as the leader until you have had an opportunity to observe the children in action and find a child who is capable of developing into a fine discussion leader. While you are acting as leader, you also have the responsibility to see that the guidelines set down by the group are strictly obeyed so that by the time a student leader takes over, the group is familiar with the rules. Some of the qualities needed by a strong discussion leader are a mind quick enough to know when to change but strong enough not to be swayed unnecessarily, a sense of timing, ability to work with people, and knowledge of the subject being discussed. It helps if the leader also has a sense of humor.

Panel discussions have an advantage over the round-table discussion because there are fewer members who are allowed to speak. The true panel discussion is carried on like a round table, using the same rules, the same type of leader, the same give-and-take. The difference lies in the number of people taking an active part. The panel usually consists of five or six people. The rest of the group are members of the audience. They are just as interested in the discussion as the panel members, but are not invited to speak until the panel discussion is over. One other advantage of the panel discussion is that the success of it does not depend so heavily upon the skill of the chairperson as it does upon the skill of each panel member.

The children have probably been taught the skill of notetaking. Notes are useful in discussion groups. Let the children refer to their

A small group of children listen as this child reads his report.

notes during a discussion but never read them. Have a planning session before the discussion and an evaluation session immediately after. The discussion should go quickly and hold attention. If it begins to drag, stop it. A discussion is a good method of exchanging ideas, facts, and opinions. Use discussions whenever they would be most effective.

Reporting is another way of sharing ideas and information, but be very careful with this method of communication. Reports can be an excellent way of sharing information without all the children having to do the same reading. A report is an excellent listening exercise for the audience. It helps the student who is giving the report gain poise and self-confidence and get the feel of an audience. It certainly provides a wonderful opportunity for locating material through reading and research, and then evaluating, organizing, and presenting the material. For reports to be effective, the teacher and the aide must plan and develop them carefully. Guard against assigning too many reports on the same day. Two is a good number, four begin to lose their effectiveness, and a roomful of reports is

This teacher aide is teaching a child to use the card catalog
to prepare a class report. To be effective, reports must be
planned and assigned carefully.

deadly. Each child should be given enough time to prepare. The
report should be scheduled and the schedule adhered to, as delay
causes tension and lessens interest. There are a variety of ways that
reporting can be done. The group should be introduced to these
ways and encouraged to use them. And again, as in almost every
learning activity, the experience should be evaluated.

This teacher aide is moderating a panel discussion. Panel
discussions help develop children's speaking skills.

To add interest to a report, the student may wish to include a map or show a homemade movie. Include songs which are relevant to the report, use interviews, demonstrate a skill, use pictures, or include skits. Various ways of evaluating reports may make them more worthwhile. For instance, a panel of students may be chosen to evaluate the reports. Role playing or creative dramatics may be used to show what the students have learned from the report.

Storytelling is another activity which children enjoy. If the aide or teacher can tell stories well, the child has a model to follow. Storytelling helps the child to learn to put ideas in sequence, to compose sentences, and to emphasize meaning with the voice. To keep this an enjoyable experience, the children need a pleasant classroom atmosphere. It should be relaxed and expectant. The child should be supported and encouraged by the aide's manner and comments.

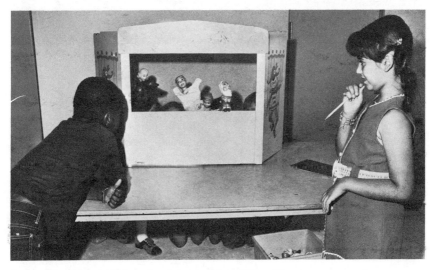

Storytelling helps children develop speaking skills. These children are using puppets to dramatize their story.

Storytelling leads directly to dramatization. Dramatization in the classroom offers a whole new opportunity for children to develop oral skills. For the very young child in the primary grades, perhaps the classroom dramatization consists of simple dramatic play. For the older child, it may consist of a large production complete with script, costumes, and sets. However, there is a whole range of dramatic experiences between these two, and they offer a variety of opportunities and skills.

Older children may use costumes, sets, and scripts to dramatize stories.

role playing   Role playing is a type of creative dramatics in
which the players take on the characteristics and problems of
members of groups other than themselves.   The purpose of role
playing is to get the child to feel the other person's point of view.
Because children can easily assume roles, they will usually get more
excited talking for others than if they were talking for themselves.
The key to the success of this experience is choosing a problem
about which there is considerable emotion.   Role playing can be effective in dealing with school or community problems, building story
values, and especially in understanding the problems in history.
Think of what an experience it would be for children to feel the emotions the California Indians experienced when the Spanish explorers
first arrived, and the problem they had in not being able to communicate with each other.   A junior high school student gains a different feeling about police officers when he or she assumes such a
role, and in the process of helping people is called a "pig."
    You may want the children to role play a situation without any
previous planning.   Other times the participants may be allowed a
little time to plan.   Only children who have knowledge of the subject and are interested in the subject should be invited to participate.

Again, do not let this experience drag on, and do not overuse it or it will not be effective when you really need it.

Other oral language activities used in the school program are telephoning, interviewing, giving announcements, directions, or explanations, conducting meetings or choral speech, and learning social conventions. The principal objectives are the same for most of these activities: building vocabulary, developing poise and ease, organizing ideas, improving research skills, building sensitivity to situations, and increasing listening skills. The adult leader can play a large part in helping the children attain these objectives by suggesting and guiding their development and evaluating kindly and meaningfully.

Children with problems must also learn oral communication skills. These problems may be disorders of articulation, retarded speech development, disorders of the voice, stuttering, and foreign language background. In the most serious cases, the child will be referred to a speech therapist. In some situations, the classroom teacher will handle the instructional procedures. In most cases, the aide will not be involved in the actual exercises but it is wise for the aide to know the nature, cause, and treatment of particular defects. Any adults working with the child should stress the production of the correct sound in their own speech. Also, the aide can help the child

Some children may need special help to develop speaking skills. For example, this aide is helping teach English to a group of Mexican-American children.

by assuming a direct, calm, objective attitude; by helping the child adjust socially to the group; by keeping the child, without pampering, from situations in which the difficulty is aggravated; and by protecting the child from the thoughtless ridicule of classmates.

Your role as an aide is a valuable one in helping the teacher and the speech therapist in the classroom. However, it is as unprofessional to attempt to remove some of these speech defects without special training as it would be to treat serious illnesses without medical training.

Listening

In recent years, a new area was added to the already overcrowded language arts curriculum. Educators felt that listening skills should be developed in a general language arts context and indeed in the total *living and learning* setting of the elementary school. It is hard to understand why it took so long for this need to be recognized. Since speaking, or oral language, has long been accepted as a skill to be developed, it stands to reason that listening, which is the complementary skill, needs to be developed. Children need to learn how to listen well just as they need to learn to speak effectively. Children vary greatly in their ability to listen, but they appear to follow the same general pattern of development. Some of the patterns are listed below:

1. Children appear to be listening but actually are grasping only limited information and are changing it to their own frame of reference.
2. Children only half listen unless it is about something in which they have a great interest.
3. Children listen passively and are easily distracted.
4. Children listen and actively react.
5. Children listen and react with evidence of genuine understanding.

One important fact for the aide to realize is that listening is a skill which needs to be learned and developed just as other skills. When children do not listen it is not always a case of poor manners, but, rather, it may be that they have never been taught to listen. Many people have the mistaken idea that listening power increases with maturity. Evidence shows that unless the child understands how to listen and has the skills which are necessary to listen effectively, maturity or incidental instruction will not make the child a critical listener.

The attitude the aide has toward listening will influence the child's success. If an aide realizes listening is a skill and treats it as such, the child will also tend to have this attitude. If it is a skill to be taught, then the teacher and the aide have a responsibility to teach the skill and to improve their own techniques and methods. Some guidelines for the aides to follow are included in this section.

Before making announcements or giving directions, give the children time to prepare to listen, then give the directions only once. To explain over and over does nothing but reinforce poor listening habits.

Say what has to be said as directly and concisely as possible. If a demonstration can be used to help children understand the explanation, use it. When your presentation is finished, ask for questions. When those are taken care of, stop and let the children work. Some educators believe learning takes place when the teacher stops talking. So let the children learn.

Be sure the children can understand the vocabulary you are using. Be perceptive to their listening mannerisms. If suddenly they appear to stop listening, think back quickly to the words you have just used. Perhaps you used a word that was not familiar to them. This is an opportunity to add to their vocabulary. Or perhaps the word has a different meaning for them. For instance, a teacher in an underprivileged area used the term juvenile literature. The children only heard the word *juvenile* and related it to *juvenile delinquency*. This had such an emotional meaning to the children that the rest of the discussion was useless as their attention could not be refocused.

Remember that listening is the intake activity. Speaking is the output activity. If children are going to be involved in the intake part, they should also be given a chance to take part in the output activity. Children will listen more willingly if they know they will have their turn to share their ideas with others who will listen to them.

There are many different listening experiences within the classroom. Most of these experiences require some kind of preparation and activities which the aide can provide to make the experience a valuable one.

A large percentage of the children's listening time is spent in listening to directions: lesson assignments, fire-drill instructions, field-trip plans, how to take a test, how to write a report, and many others. Since children have to listen to directions so often, aides should work to give directions clearly.

These precautions will guarantee better listening habits or at least better attention from the students. Before you begin giving directions, prepare in this way:

1. Make sure that you realize just what it is you want the children to do and then plan your directions so that they are clear and easily understood by the children.
2. If you are reading or explaining someone else's directions, make sure that you understand what the children are to do before you try to explain it to them.
3. Have the attention of the children before you start giving directions. Don't start until the children that you are addressing are in their places and ready to listen. One child moving around and putting things away can distract most of the other children in the group.
4. Speak in a clear voice, loud enough to be heard easily but not so loud that the volume detracts from the purpose.
5. Start with clear simple directions; build up to the more complicated ones.
6. Do not interrupt your directions by irrelevant comments.
7. If possible, demonstrate your directions by showing an example of a drawing, a picture, or a diagram on the board. Sometimes it is possible to include a word picture in your explanation which will help the child develop a mental picture.

When teachers or aides present an oral lesson to the children, they should keep these points in mind:

1. The material must be in keeping with the child's interests and ability to understand.
2. Before presenting an oral lesson, it is necessary to find out what the child already knows about the subject. Perhaps it is not necessary to include such a wide range of information.
3. Sometimes in a listening lesson, it is possible to include visual aids to help the child get a mental picture. For instance, before a child sees a film on a certain country, it may be helpful to locate that country on the classroom map and discuss the geographical location.
4. Before the lesson begins, tell the children what the topic is going to be and ask them what they think they might find out about it from this lesson.
5. Suggest things that they might listen for. If the lesson is going to be presented in a certain organizational pattern, call this to their attention.
6. When the lesson is over, bring the children together and list on the

board or chart the things they learned from the film. Group these ideas into categories. If students are able, help them generalize what they have learned. Some students may be able to evaluate the lesson.

Other listening opportunities may be: listening for pleasure, listening to analyze, listening to conversations, listening to the power of the spoken word, listening to create, and listening for cues. All these areas are important. The same directions you have learned to use with previously mentioned listening activities will help with these.

Children learn from discussion that good listeners are polite, get the facts, listen thoughtfully, listen for a reason, and make intelligent use of what they hear.

Writing

Writing is a communication skill which can be divided into the following components: handwriting, practical writing, creative writing, and spelling. This section will treat each area individually.

Both manuscript and cursive writing are taught in the elementary schools. Manuscript writing is generally regarded as more desirable for use by first- and second-grade children. It is more legible and easier for the children to write and to read since it is similar to the print in the book. Manuscript writing consists of unjoined letters made with lines and circles. In cursive writing the letters are joined together and written in a running hand. Samples of manuscript and cursive letters are shown on pages 60 and 61. For some children, the transition from manuscript printing to cursive writing is an easy one which they look forward to with much anticipation. In fact, many children will begin trying cursive writing before it has been formally taught. For others, the challenge of learning a new form of writing is so overwhelming that the complete changeover takes several years and sometimes it is never accomplished. If this is so, you may wonder why the school bothers to make the change. Cursive writing is a faster method of writing than manuscript writing. Handwriting has a direct correlation with small-muscle coordination, so progress is a very individual thing. You cannot expect the complete class to progress at the same speed. It would be wise for aides to discuss this area with their teachers to see what the handwriting objectives are for their students.

In many programs, the child first learns to write by copying a model. The teacher shows how the letters are formed and calls

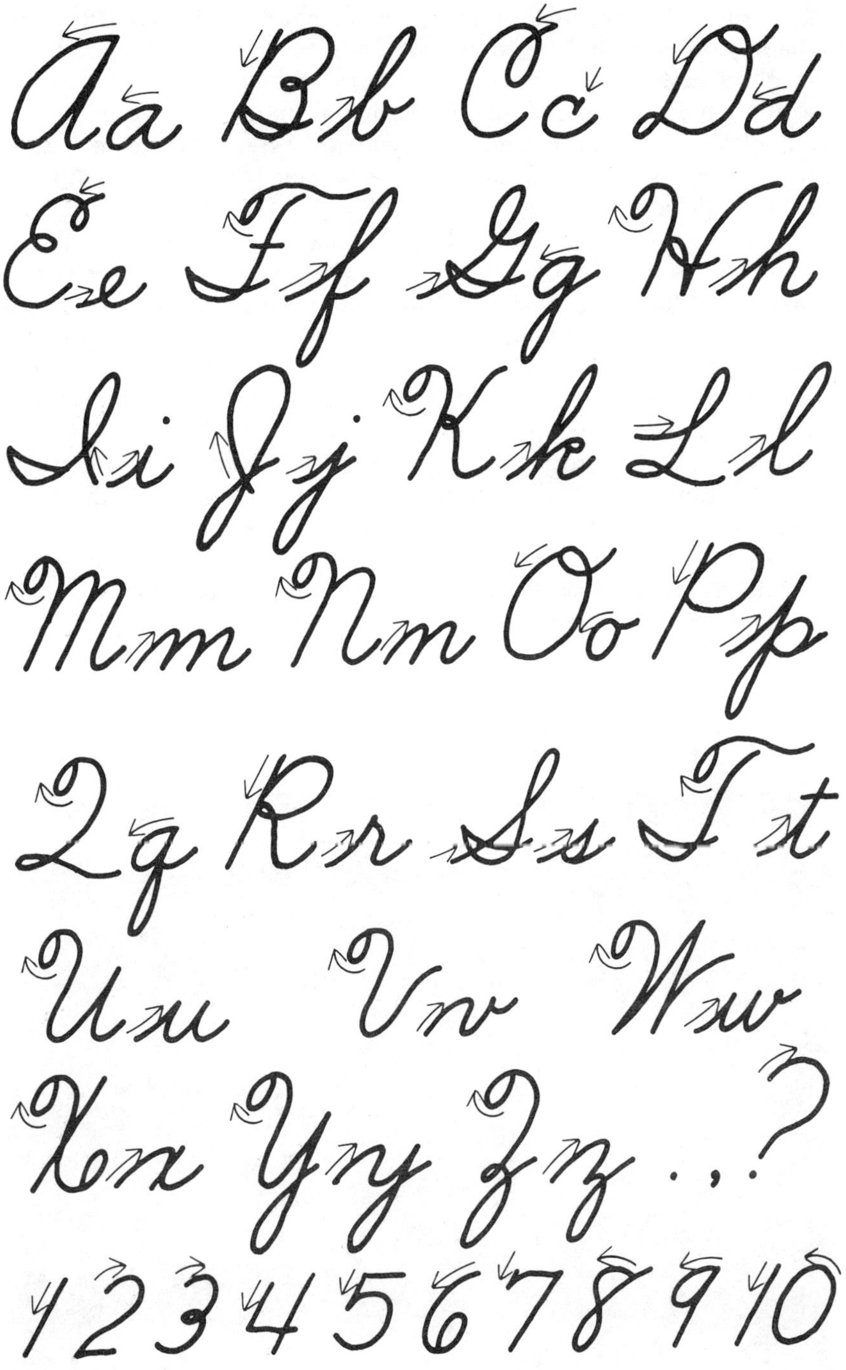

Aa Bb Cc Dd
Ee Ff Gg Hh
Ii Jj Kk Ll
Mm Nn Oo Pp
Qq Rr Ss Tt
Uu Vv Ww
Xx Yy Zz . , ?
1 2 3 4 5 6 7 8 9 10

attention to the spacing, and then goes from child to child to help. What a wonderful help if there is an aide to share this duty. When the child first learns manuscript writing, the teacher will use the writing paper designated for the particular grade level being taught and will also use larger pencils. If you are asked to take care of supplies, be sure you are informed as to what size paper and pencils the teacher will need.

At the end of the second grade, many children show a real eagerness to begin cursive writing. Some teachers feel this is the time to start teaching cursive writing to the class. Others feel that it should be started in the fall term of the third grade so the children do not practice without supervision during the summer months. Whenever cursive writing is taught, it is usually started gradually and should conform to the principle of moving from the simple to the complex. The lowercase letters are usually introduced first and the capital letters are usually introduced in association with the children's names. As in manuscript writing, there is special ruled paper for this. Because children have a tendency to write very small when they begin cursive writing, the paper usually has light and very heavy alternating lines. Be sure, if you are going to help the children, you know how the paper is used.

This child is practicing cursive writing. Note how her paper is slanted as she prepares to write.

Slant of the letters is important in cursive writing. Slant and the joining of letters are the main differences between cursive and manuscript writing. When children are practicing this, their paper should be slanted on the desk in front of them. If the child is right-handed, the paper should slant to the left with the bottom corner pointing toward the heart. If the child is left-handed, the paper should slant to the right.

If the aide is to help during the handwriting activity, he or she should know the standards for handwriting. These are:

1. The letter sizes should be the same height. When practicing handwriting, the small letters should be one-half space tall and the tall letters the full space.
2. All letters must slant the same way at the same angle.
3. All letters should sit on the base line.
4. The spaces between the words should be even.
5. The humps on *m, n, h, v,* and *y* should be rounded.
6. The retrace lines on *i, d, t, m,* and *n* should be retraced.
7. Loops on *f, g, h, k, l, y,* and *b* should be well formed.
8. The letters *a, d, g, o, p,* and *s* should be closed.
9. All downstrokes should be straight.
10. The endings of words should have strong ending strokes.

The left-handed child often finds writing frustrating, but with help and preplanning by the adults in the classroom it need not be. First of all, children are entitled to write with their left hand. You should know the ways of helping them do it well. First, the fact that they are left-handed should not be accentuated. Next, the seating arrangement for left-handed children should be planned because if they are seated next to right-handed children, they will bump arms constantly. Sometimes left-handed children are grouped together. However, if this is done, it must be done without making the left-handed children feel different. When the child begins slanted cursive writing, a left-handed child will slant the paper in the opposite direction from the right-handed child.

Many left-handed children prefer vertical writing. Check with your teacher and see how this is to be handled. Many left-handed children, if slanting is required, may begin writing backhanded. The objective of writing is legibility and ease of writing. Backhanded writing is not easily legible.

writing composition In most classrooms, written composition is broken into two main categories: practical writing and creative writing. Perhaps when introduced in the classroom these writing techniques are developed separately and serve different purposes, but the children gradually carry over the techniques they learned in practical writing and apply them in their personal writing.

Practical writing is done in any situation in which there is need for it. Writing of this type is to be read by people other than the writer, and therefore must be written so that it can be read easily. Here the emphasis may be placed upon the mechanics of writing: spelling, penmanship, neatness, punctuation, and other external items. This type of writing includes such activities as invitations, notes, letters, reports, and, to some degree, newspaper items and interviews. In practical writing the teacher furnishes whatever guidance the child is ready for and can use.

Creative writing is writing that is basically done for the writer's own satisfaction, although it may be shared with others. Creative or imaginative writing includes writing of stories, poems, and plays—anything that the child wishes to express. Here the emphasis is placed on getting the child's ideas down in such a way that they represent the writer and his or her thinking.

Which type of writing does the school emphasize? It is not a case of pushing creative writing versus practical writing. It is a case of encouraging the child to say something that is worth saying and saying it effectively.

Before children can write, they need something to write about. They need to feel that they want to express themselves, that they have something to say that others would be interested in. Many times it is necessary for the schools to provide some type of experience for children before they are asked to write. For example, sometimes children who have never shown any interest in sharing their thoughts with others have written enthusiastically about the classroom pet whose care has been their responsibility. Field trips provide another stimulus for writers. When you are helping children in composition classes, remember that they need a subject that they can relate to before they can ever begin to put their ideas on paper.

Sometimes being taught writing skills can absolutely kill the child's desire to write. However, young writers have to know the mechanics of writing so their meaning is safeguarded. But mechanical writing skills must be introduced in a very positive and encouraging manner. For instance, if children are taught punctuation by having their compositions returned with red marks slashed through paragraphs, words crossed out, and comments such as: Watch your punctuation, or I don't understand you, in the margin, they are not going to be too anxious to try writing again. If they do write, their minds are going to be so taken up with watching their punctuation, that their writing will be stilted. Yet mechanics of good writing are needed.

Children can be introduced to the mechanics of writing at the same time as they begin reading. When the child first comes across a question mark in the primer, the teacher points out that this is a question mark and it is used when the speaker wants an answer. This continues throughout the grades. Along with this, the teacher and the aide will work with the children in their writing. Many children have this pattern of writing their stories: First they get their ideas down on paper without worrying about the mechanics, then they meet with someone who will help them make the mechanical corrections. They know that to be understood, they must follow certain rules, and they will gladly make the mechanical corrections as long as the adult who is helping them understands that pattern and provides the help and encouragement needed. Often it will help to let the children read their writing to you aloud. When they do this, it becomes obvious where there are pauses that require a comma or a period, where a question mark should be, and what words should be in quotation marks.

But the mechanics of writing are not taught only during creative writing lessons. Very often they are presented in practices which have a single objective—for example, putting capital letters on the names of all cities included in a written paragraph. At the end of this practice, other practices will be used to reinforce this concept. This method can be used in teaching punctuation, capitalization, letter writing, grammar, outlining, and reporting. The aide who knows these mechanics and also has a few games up his or her sleeve to help the children enjoy this learning will certainly be a welcome member of the classroom staff.

Before an aide attempts to help a child in any written work, the teacher's or classroom's rules for the manuscript form must be known. Although there are no set rules, the teacher usually establishes the form for the class. To avoid confusion, ask the teacher what form is favored, or ask if the school has a certain form for the guidance of teachers and pupils.

Punctuation is a necessary skill in written expression. An unlimited number of punctuation rules exist without too much agreement as to the importance of each one. However, there are suggested lists of punctuation items that should be taught in the elementary schools. If children are taught these rules, then the aides certainly need to know them to reinforce the teaching. If you are not overly confident of them, take home one of the English textbooks and brush up on the rules.

Capitalization, like punctuation, is a mechanical element of written language. Many rules exist which deal with capitalization. In addition to reinforcing the proper use of capital letters, training must be directed toward the importance of eliminating unnecessary capitals in writing. In particular, the practice of capitalizing words for purposes of emphasis should be avoided.

outlining Simple outlines are first introduced in the primary grades as either a part of language or learning instruction. Thus children learn early the idea of classification and organization. Simple outlines may be used for such things as a story to be told or dramatized, a trip that is to be taken or was taken, materials needed for a project, or activity plans for a project. Outlines are taught in greater detail in the intermediate grades.

Outlines may be made in topical form or in sentence form. For the younger children, the sentence form is easier to follow. The important thing for children to learn is to use one form consistently within the same outline. There is no one acceptable form for outlining. Therefore, if you are assigned to work with a group of children in an outlining lesson, be familiar with the form the teacher is using.

reports Written language programs include writing of summaries, directions, and reviews, as well as the writing of reports. This type of writing is important in carrying out the activities which generally make up a part of social sciences and science programs in the school.

After the children have written their reports, some editing will have to be done. This is very often the aide's duty. Before you take on this duty, though, you should know what standards the class and the teacher have developed. The standards may include such things as:

1. Title of the report should be written in the center of the line. Skip a line after the title.
2. Begin the first word of the title with a capital letter. Capitalize each important word of the title.

3. Have adequate margins at the top, bottom, left, and right.
4. Use clear, neat writing.
5. Use correct spelling and punctuation.
6. Have sentence sense. Do not use incomplete, run-on, or choppy sentences.
7. Indent all paragraphs.
8. Sign your name at the bottom of the last page.

To help you in checking reports, you might use editing signs. These signs could be displayed on a chart so the children could understand their meaning. Perhaps the teacher has developed some of these with the class. Or the teacher may have his or her own system. Ask before you begin. Some suggested ones are:

sp = spelling
cap = capital letter
lc = lowercase letter
p = wrong punctuation
. , ; : = add punctuation
inc = incomplete sentence
¶ = start new paragraph
no ¶ = no new paragraph
= insert space
? = unclear
mb = margins too big
ms = margins too small

Teachers carefully divide children into reading groups according to ability, plan their lessons with individual achievement in mind, and provide many reading experiences. Yet they will teach spelling using the same book for all children on the same time schedule. Why do they do this? Probably because individualizing any class takes time and more personnel. Since spelling does not elicit the same demands from the community as reading and math, reading and math get the emphasis. Most people have the feeling that children do not need much guidance from the teacher in spelling, and that the home can share responsibility for the spelling program. If the spelling program consisted only of studying a list of words and being tested on that list perhaps this would be true. However, a good spelling program is more than that.

The complete spelling program includes listening, speech, writing, and work analysis skills. These skills are not developed by giving children a list of words and testing the children five days later. Words need to be introduced. Sounds, syllables, meanings, structural patterns, pronunciations, and phonetic aids are pointed out so the children become familiar with many different aspects of the words.

No matter what type of spelling program the school uses, dictionaries can be used as part of the program. Young children may use a very simplified dictionary such as the one shown here.

Three main types of spelling programs exist. Each of these programs use different methods of teaching spelling. Some schools use the regular hardback spelling book which contains lists of spelling words and, in some cases, some spelling help with each list. In the second type of program, classes use a spelling workbook. The lists of words are introduced, and then several different learning activities are used with each lesson. The third program consists of the teacher choosing words that the children need for writing and also the ones they misspell the most. This can be highly individualized with the teacher choosing the words for each child from the writing the child has done. Each child may have a different list, or one list may be used for the entire class. Some classes have all three programs going on at the same time for different children.

With an aide in the classroom, it is now becoming possible to set up individualized spelling programs. Some children have such good spelling sense that very often they pass a pretest and should be able to go on. Others need the usual time, about a week, to complete their lesson. Still others cannot learn the whole list at one time even if they have a month to work on it. But if someone can work with these children so they learn just five words a day, by the end of the week they may have the whole list mastered. Still other children are not working at their grade level; they may need a program for the grade above or below them, they may need an enriched or remedial program, or perhaps they may need a closer diagnosis as to what their problem is. Perhaps they are not hearing the sounds, perhaps they cannot write fast enough to keep up, or perhaps they have failed at spelling so long they are not trying anymore.

As a classroom aide chances are great that you will be assigned to give spelling tests. If you have an opportunity to observe the teacher doing this before you are called upon to take over this task, watch to see what the teacher's patterns and techniques are. Perhaps they will work for you. Below are some suggestions to help you.

Be sure you enunciate the words clearly. Be especially careful that you do not leave off endings.

Allow enough time for the children to write the word, but not so much that the children's minds begin to wander as they wait for you to go on.

Try the following method for a word test: Say the word, use it in a sentence, repeat the word, and then be quiet and let them write. Do not use this time to discuss the word, make suggestions to children, or anything else. Children need quiet to bring the image of the word back into their minds.

If the test is a dictation sentence test, read the complete sentence first. Break the sentence into phrases and read a phrase. Allow the children time to write the phrase. Read another phrase, and again allow writing time. Continue this until the sentence is completed. Then repeat the entire sentence. Ask, at that time, if anyone needs any part of that sentence repeated. Go on to the next sentence. Remember the rule that neither you nor the children talk while they are writing the phrases. If they need your help, ask that they raise their hands and go to them and converse in whispering tones so other children are not disturbed. In most cases, if you make it clear to the children that you will repeat the complete sentence, they can wait with their request for help.

Move about during the test. While you are doing this, you can observe the children's writing speed, their thinking techniques, the real spelling puzzlers.

Remember that the seventy-five minutes or so of spelling instruction a week is not the whole spelling program. Spelling goes on all day. Spelling skills overlap reading, writing, listening, and grammar skills. The success of the spelling program is not measured by whether children get perfect scores every week on a list of words, but rather by whether they are able to transfer their spelling skills to their writing and reading activities.

creative writing   What is creative writing?   The explanation of creative writing varies. Creative expression should not be confused with the teaching of writing techniques. However, the two should work to enhance each other. With writing, spelling, and grammar skills, creative writing becomes more possible for children. By using these skills, they see that other people are able to enjoy their ideas, and so they are motivated to produce more. However, most teachers will feel that writing rules should not get in the way of creative thoughts.

The fact that creativity cannot be taught has made teachers wonder: If it cannot be taught, then how can I help my students? What methods should I use? How do I plan for their needs? How does creative writing develop through the years? The aide also needs this information in order to provide the help that is needed.

The aide helps children compose stories during creative writing. A child may draw a picture as part of the story.

Before children begin to write, they share their creative experience either by painting a picture or by telling someone about it, perhaps the teacher, the aide, or the entire class. Soon the teacher begins writing these stories on chart paper. Sometimes the whole class helps to make up the story. Sometimes the story belongs to just one child. As the children watch their spoken word transformed into a pattern of letters, they begin putting words together on paper to share with others. The words may not be spelled correctly, but they are accepted readily by the adults in the classroom because the objective is to get the children to express themselves by writing. This plan grows during the primary grades. The children experience some kind of a happening. They think about it and discuss it together and then are given the opportunity to express themselves freely in writing. The teacher may lead the discussion and put up words on the board that the children are using in their discussion. Then they begin writing. Now the aide will move around the room helping supply the correct spelling for words that are not there. This is no time to conduct a spelling lesson. Give them the spelling of a word as soon as they ask for it so that they can get back to their writing. (You may want to jot the word down so you can work with them later.) Some teachers provide their students with composition books for their own individual dictionaries. When a child asks about the spelling of a word, the teacher or the aide writes the word in the correct alphabetical place in their book.

To begin with, the teacher or the aide probably will not get too upset with errors. The stories will contain misspelled words, fragmented sentences, and either an overabundance of punctuation marks or maybe none at all. After the children have written many stories and do so with ease, then the teacher or the aide and child correct the first rough draft together. As an aide coming into a classroom, you may be quite concerned with all these errors and no one correcting them. You may be tempted to ask, as many parents do, When will these children be expected to spell and write correctly? Many educators feel that sometime during the late second or early third grade, the children begin to see the correct form. Perhaps these new standards are the result of wide reading and gradual mastery of writing mechanics.

The creative writing program differs a little in the intermediate grades. The sequence is that of motivation, skill development, refinement, and use. The object of writing does not need to be a story. Frequently the purpose is to help children write with vividness and insight. The material may be a story, report, autobiography, dramatic play, sketch, poem, or newspaper item. The point is that the child is learning to express ideas effectively in writing.

A story formula will challenge some children and provide guidelines for others. A good story has five parts: a beginning, a problem, a high point or climax, a following action or solution, and a satisfactory ending. A chart may be used to check the formula. These five points may be put on a chart and used by the children to check their stories.

To assign creative writing to some children is like opening a faucet. Writing pours out. Some children just seem to be alert to the details of the world in which they live. Others need a great amount of help and encouragement. Educators who work with children in the area of creative writing have found that although you cannot teach children to write creatively, you can help them to express the original ideas they have. Behind the story, poem, or letter, behind the clear, concise sentence or the stumbling search for words, is the child and all that she or he can become. Creative writing is one more way to understand the child.

Reading

It is impossible in such a brief chapter to tell an instructional aide everything that is needed to help a teacher teach reading. The libraries are full of books suggesting different methods to use. The classrooms are full of guidebooks and teaching aids for reading. The teacher is probably better prepared to teach reading than any other part of the curriculum. If this is so, then perhaps this part of the chapter should be skipped completely. Not at all. Aides are much used in reading programs. Considering the need for aides in reading programs and the overabundance of material to help them, this book needs to stress understanding reading goals. If the aide knows the reading goals, the teacher has a starting point from which to begin work with the aide.

Methods of teaching reading have gone through many different stages, and consequently the concept of reading itself has changed. Educators have moved from the idea that reading merely involves recognizing letter symbols (phonetics) to the present-day concept that thinking is a component part of reading. In reading, the child brings meaning to the printed symbols. The meaning comes from different experiences the child has had. Learning to read is no longer thought of as mastering a bag of tricks which can be learned through repetition and practice. Learning to read is now recognized as one of the most important and most difficult of all the developmental tasks the child is called upon to achieve. In our culture, the child is expected

In an individualized reading plan children may be asked to
choose their own reading materials. The aide may be
responsible for varying the available books.

not only to be able to read, but to want to read. It is not just a skill;
it is a resource for fuller living.

As the thinking about what reading is has changed, so has the
thinking about whose responsibility it is to teach reading. No longer
do the primary grades alone have this task. The responsibility is a
lifetime task.

Why is it that some children become so keenly interested in
reading that they practically teach themselves to read while others
require a great deal of motivation and guidance over a long period of
time just to begin reading? Many reasons have been offered for this.
One reason is that when reading is part of the family living experience, children learn faster. Also, when children have had many
varied experiences, they adapt to reading faster.

Schools found out a long time ago that not every child learns
the same way and that not every teacher is effective with the same

The aide may help children select appropriate reading material in a programmed reading plan.

teaching method. Many different accepted ways of teaching reading are available. Maybe these came about by teachers searching for a way to provide each child with a way of learning. Many different ways may be used in one classroom. Such methods may be in the basal text, the language experience, the selective reading program, a variety of programmed reading plans, the I.T.A. (Initial Teaching Alphabet) Reading Alphabet, and many others. When you first meet with your teacher, ask which method is being used. You will more than likely be provided with materials to help you understand that plan's objective and methods.

Earlier it was suggested that teacher aides provide much help in the reading program. How, then, are teacher aides used?

In the very early grades, the children are encouraged to write stories in connection with their reading. This is especially true in the language arts approach to reading. One teacher cannot possibly get around to the whole class as often as is needed. But two pairs of hands can make the job lighter, and yours is the second pair of hands. To carry out this assignment, you must know the correct form of manuscript letters. Remember that the child is learning writing skills as he or she writes the story. If you do not know the correct form of manuscript letters, refer to the writing sample in this chapter (page 60) and practice. Talk with your teacher about other points to be stressed, such as margins, capital letters, punctuation and spacing. The teacher may have a particular method of introducing and reinforcing these concepts. The teacher may also have a definite schedule for introducing these concepts. Usually you can reinforce writing skills by talking about them, pointing out any changes, and perhaps explaining to the child why you are making changes. However, writing does need to be reinforced at every opportunity. Another important part of this teaching experience is the opportunity it gives you as an adult to give the child your full attention. Give the children the idea that at that time they are the most important persons in your life, that you are happy to be able to work with them, and that you think their story is the best you have ever read. Praise them on their sentence form, their choice of words, or whatever else you find to praise.

Reading games teach children new skills and help them review skills. An aide is often responsible for constructing, supervising, and distributing these games.

During reading and at many other times during the day, the teacher may post on a bulletin board the words used most often by the children. Very often the teacher may use a *word ladder* which is a list of words. Perhaps word charts may also be used. Word charts may list words under certain subjects, such as circus words, family words, math words, and others that may be needed along with a unit which is being studied. Again, if you know how to form manuscript letters properly, you may be asked to write the word cards and charts and keep them current.

In a primary class where the teacher is using the basal reader approach, you may also be asked to write word cards. The teacher may use them when introducing the story. The children may use them afterwards as flash cards to reinforce their reading vocabularies. Some schools buy commercial word cards with the basal text, so do not make word cards until you are sure they are needed. A teacher may want a set made for a certain child to take home for practice. Board or chart presentations are used extensively in the basal text approach. Words or sentences may need to be written before class time. Perfect your board manuscript and offer to take over this job.

Teachers often use a cassette or tape recorder to tape the story or to record questions about the story. Many times this is the aide's responsibility. If you are not sure about how to use cassettes or tape recorders, let the chapter on audiovisual aids help you. After you have read the chapter, experiment with a recorder.

Basal text reading continues on into the intermediate grades, and in many cases the needs are similar to the primary grades. However, methods, materials, and objectives change as skills grow. More reference books are needed. Higher levels of thinking are being developed. Children are beginning to show definite preference in their reading material. Teacher aides are kept busy gathering the reference materials the teacher needs, providing worksheets the teacher has assigned, keeping records on the children's growth in skills, and giving special attention to those few who need primary skills.

In the intermediate grades, you will very often find children in a programmed reading plan. In this method, the child can work quite independently. The reading material, the evaluation tools, and the record-keeping charts are all provided for the student's use. However, this program, like every other one, works best when the student can share success with someone. You can also provide help when and if it is needed and also watch for progress.

As children grow, their range of interests, abilities, and skills broaden in one classroom. The teacher gets frustrated trying to reach the needs of all the children. Many teachers turn to the individualized or selective reading program. The biggest drawback to this is the time-consuming task of meeting with each child often enough and making that meeting worthwhile to both teacher and student. Here is another opportunity for the aide to fill a tremendous need in the classroom. The aide could take care of alternate conferences. During this time, the children will come to you, read a portion of the book that they have selected, and then the two of you will discuss it. Watch for signs of tension, visual problems, speech problems. Make sure the child has chosen a book which is suited to his or her reading level. This is another opportunity for the child to have the full attention of an adult for a period of time, and although it may be just a short period, it is a very important one. Make it important for the child. Do what you can to provide motivation. Keep your help and comments positive. Praise the child but remember, at this age the praise must be valid and the giving of it sincere.

One of the purposes of these conferences is to give children an opportunity to develop their thoughts as they talk about the story. Ask questions which will cause the child to recall the facts, make inferences, come to some kind of a generalization, put the facts in sequence, and be aware of feelings and attitudes. Some possible questions for conferences are these:

1. What was the setting of the story? Where did the story take place?
2. What was the time or period of the story or book? In what year did the people live?
3. What were some of the personality differences among the various characters in the book? Which characters were happy, sad, kind, mean?
4. How did the story make you feel—angry, excited, afraid?
5. If you were one of the characters in the story, would you have done what he or she did?
6. What was the story about? Did the action build up as you were reading? Was the story told in flashback form?
7. What was your reaction to the hero? Did you admire the hero or dislike him or her? Were you satisfied with what the hero did?
8. Which one of the characters in the story did you identify with or admire most? Which one did you like least? Why?
9. What did you learn from the book that you didn't know before?
10. Has the book suggested other kinds of things that you would like to look for to read?

When teachers were asked how they would use aides in their language arts programs, they gave many suggestions. One that came up very often was to have aides make language arts learning games and use them with groups of children. Children love learning games, and they are effective in reinforcing skills. Games do take time to construct and usually they require some supervision. Where can you find these games? The sources are numerous. The professional library may have books on games. The professional magazines will include games each month. College bookstores have books of learning games. Every teacher has materials on games which have been picked up at workshop meetings. Many of the most successful games are those made up from variations of other games.

Methods and materials are important elements in teaching reading, but perhaps another, just as important, is the teacher's and the aide's attitudes toward the subject and the child.

The most important assignment of the elementary school is to teach children to read. This does not mean to be able to call out words, but to use reading in their learning and for their enjoyment. If children are learning to read and are enthusiastic readers, the

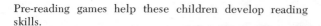

Pre-reading games help these children develop reading skills.

school will be supported by the public. If they are not learning to read, public support turns to criticism. Perhaps this is as it should be because the public knows that without reading skills, all areas of the curriculum will suffer. This is a tremendous responsibility and one that all school people share.

The attitude toward the child in the reading program is either going to help or hinder progress, depending on the teacher's, the aide's, and the children's attitudes toward each reading experience. If ever a child needs help and encouragement, this is the time. Be very careful of the comments you make, your facial expressions, the materials you offer. Do what you can to keep that preschool enthusiasm for reading strong when the child passes through your grade.

Chapter Summary

Language arts skills include all skills necessary for communication. Speaking, listening, writing, and reading are the main skills involved.

Speaking skills need to be developed systematically if the child is to develop into a good conversationalist. A good conversationalist should have a variety of interests, be a good listener, use examples for illustration, have the ability to read clues, and know when to stop talking. Along with this, other qualities necessary for effective speaking are: pleasant voice, good posture, articulation, and acceptable grammar. Poise and ease usually come with the feeling of adequacy in speaking. All the qualities of speech not only need to be learned, but also need to be practiced. Some of the activities in which speaking skills may be developed are: (1) small-group discussion, (2) panel discussions, (3) reports, (4) demonstrations, (5) skits, (6) storytelling, (7) role playing and other dramatizations, (8) telephoning, (9) conducting meetings, and (10) interviewing. These activities will also be helpful in building vocabulary, organizing ideas, improving resource skills, building sensitivity to situations, and increasing listening skills.

Listening skills vary greatly for different children and need to be learned. Children need to be made aware that listening is a skill that needs to be developed, and it will not come naturally with maturity. Some common practices that may be used to help develop listening skills are: (1) Before making announcements or giving directions, make sure the children are prepared to listen and then give them the directions only once. (2) Be sure the directions are clear and concise. (3) Be sure to use vocabulary the children understand. (4) Give the children a chance to present their ideas after they have listened to the ideas of others. (5) Remind them that a good listener is polite, gets the facts, listens thoughtfully, listens for a reason, and makes intelligent use of what he or she hears.

Writing skills may be divided into four component parts: (1) handwriting, (2) factual writing, (3) creative writing, and (4) spelling.

Both manuscript and cursive writing are taught in the elementary schools. Manuscript writing is taught first with cursive writing following as children develop small-muscle control and coordination. The aide may be most helpful in helping children practice their writing skills if aware of the standards of handwriting the teacher is using. Correcting a child before a mistake is repeated is most important. The aide, with proper training, should be able to spot quickly the obvious mistakes children normally make and guide them to use the correct procedure.

Practical writing deals with the mechanics of writing. Spelling, penmanship, punctuation, and other external items are emphasized. Included in this type of writing are letters, invitations, notes, reports, and other such items where the students are being taught correctly to write effectively.

Creative writing is basically for the writers themselves although they may share it with others. Creative writing and practical or technical writing are two different things. Techniques of writing are comparatively easy to teach. Creative writing needs to be facilitated rather than taught. Guidelines need to be established to help children create and express themselves effectively. An example of the guidelines is the requirement of the five component parts of a good story which are: (1) a beginning, (2) a problem, (3) a high point, (4) a following action or solution, and (5) a satisfactory ending. Children vary greatly in their ability to write creatively. Some require a great deal of help to get them to express their original ideas while others literally pour out their ideas in writing. Motivation plays an extremely important part in getting the child to write creatively.

Reading skills are the most important and difficult developmental task the child must achieve. The concept of reading has changed from the phonetic recognition of a letter symbol to the present-day concept that thinking is a component part of reading. It is not enough that children learn to read. They must also want to read if they are to use this resource for a fuller life.

Suggested References

Allen, Roach Van, and Allen, Claryce. *Language Experiences in Reading.* Chicago: Encyclopedia Britannica Press, 1967.

Anderson, Paul S. *Language Skills in Elementary Education.* New York: The Macmillan Company, 1964.

Applegate, Maureen. *Easy in English.* Evanston, Illinois: Harper and Row Publishers, Incorporated, 1963.

Arbuthnot, May Hill. *Children and Books,* rev. ed. Chicago: Scott, Foresman and Company, 1968.

Arbuthnot, May Hill. *The Arbuthnot Anthology of Children's Literature,* 3d. ed. New York: Lothrop, Lee & Shepard Co., Inc., 1971.

Bloomer, Richard H. *Skill Games to Teach Reading.* Dansville, New York: The Instructor (pamphlet), 1969.

Forte, Imogene, Frank, Marjorie, and Mackenzie, Joy. *Kid's Stuff—Reading and Language Experience—Intermediate-Jr. High.* Nashville, Tennessee: Incentive Publications, 1973.

Forte, Imogene and Mackenzie, Joy. *Nooks, Crannies and Corners: Learning Centers for Creative Classrooms.* Nashville, Tennessee: Incentive Publications, 1972.

Gigous, G. M. *Improving Listening Skills.* Dansville, New York: The Instructor (pamphlet), 1967.

Green, Harry A., and Petty, Walter T. *Developing Language Skills in the Elementary School.* Boston: Allyn and Bacon, Inc., 1961.

Hurwitz, Abraham B., and Goddard, Arthur. *Games to Improve Your Child's English.* New York: Simon and Schuster, Inc., 1969.

Jacobs, Leland B., et al. *Individualizing Reading Practices.* New York: Columbia University, Teachers College Press, 1958.

Jennings, Frank G. *This Is Reading.* New York: Columbia University, Teachers College Press, 1965.

Noble, J. Kendrick. *Handwriting for Everyday Use.* Sacramento: California State Department of Education, 1959.

Russell, David H. *Children Learn to Read.* Boston: Ginn and Company, 1949.

Tinker, Miles A., and McCullough, Constance M. *Teaching Elementary Reading.* New York: Appleton-Century Crofts, Inc., Meredith Press, 1968.

Introduction

Science and the social sciences overlap in content, depend on each other, and enrich each other. The following fields of study—anatomy, history, biology, psychology, sociology, and even geography—are interrelated. A knowledge of one area gives insight into the other areas. Even though some of these areas are classified as *pure* science (anatomy and biology) while the others are *social* sciences, we see evidence of the fusion of the two in such areas as ecology, technology, and economics. It follows, then, that educators have a great responsibility in providing learning experiences which show children what each of these subject areas is like and how the larger fields of science and the social sciences are related.

Teaching methods in these subject areas have changed greatly. In the past, a teacher was likely to assign students a number of pages to read in the textbook, and then the students would answer questions at the end of the chapter. The discussion which followed was a review of what the children had read. As more was discovered about the ways in which children learn, it became apparent that although they did acquire facts by using this method, they were not able to apply the principles of what they had learned. Educators began to realize that both children and adults learn better by being actively involved in what they are learning. For instance, how does one learn to swim or ride a bike unless one actually swims or rides? In the same way a child learns to write stories by writing stories, learns to recognize the principles of democracy by living in a democracy, and learns to think by having the opportunity to solve thought-provoking problems.

As children began to be more actively involved in new kinds of learning situations, especially those involving problem solving, it became obvious that not all children were prepared to solve the problems presented. Some children could draw on knowledge they already had and could apply it to solving a problem. Other children were even able to predict what would happen next. Some were even ready to apply certain of their own values to the situation. However, some were not able to do any of these things.

Development of Problem-Solving Skills

While trying to create a plan for teaching problem-solving skills, educators concluded that there are definite levels of thinking involved in problem solving. Researchers have not all

social sciences and science   3

agreed on the number of levels there are or on how to label each level, but all have come up with the same basic description of these levels.   Barnes and Burgdorf in their book, *New Approaches to Teaching Elementary Social Studies,* state that problem solving in elementary social studies will ordinarily involve six levels.   These levels are (1) *identifying* the problem, (2) *clarifying* the problem, (3) *collecting data* relevant to the problem, (4) *analyzing and organizing* the data collected, (5) *determining possible solutions,* and (6) *evaluating the solutions* which appear to hold most promise.[1]

It may be helpful here to discuss each level and suggest ways in which the teacher-and-aide team may use them.   The first, identifying the problem, is not too difficult because the problems are usually obvious from the material being studied.   For example, the overall problem, might be "the Civil War."   Solving the problem will probably require the use of other materials such as related books, audiovisual equipment, materials for experimenting, resource people, etc.   Therefore, when children choose or are given problems to solve, it is important that the teacher and aide know what kinds of materials will be needed and make a variety of materials available to the children.   Sometimes, problem solving is more interesting and more meaningful if more than one child is working on the problem.   A student may choose a partner and work together on the problem, or the problem may be assigned to a committee of students.   Remind the students that completing class assignments—a written or oral report or a project showing the conclusions reached within the assigned time limit—is part of the problem.

The second step is clarifying the problem.   It will help the students to encourage them to break up the big problem into subproblems.   To start them on this, you may get them to think about *who, what, where, why,* and *how* questions.   *Who* is concerned, *what* is happening, and *why* is it a problem?   For example, students may choose to examine the causes of the Civil War, the reasons that particular states chose the side they did, the reasons for the rise of particular leaders, etc.

Now that the problem is broken down, it is time for students to move on to the next step, which is collecting data.   If there is a committee, the task can be divided among its members.   At this point, the teacher is going to be concerned about the kinds of research skills the children are using.   If children do not know how to use the

---

[1]   Barnes, Donald L., and Burgdorf, Arlene B.   *New Approaches to Teaching Elementary Social Studies.*   Minneapolis: Burgess Publishing Co., 1969.

needed reference materials, this is the time to help them learn. As children first begin to acquire this skill, it might be helpful to list some reference materials they will use and even to give page numbers to some students. As the skills grow, less direction will be required. The following is one useful method of collecting data: Give the children small slips of paper. Ask them to write down facts on these slips of paper which they feel are important in solving the problem. Direct them to write the name of the source where they found this fact on the backs of the papers. Be sure to emphasize that they are to write just one fact on one slip of paper. This is to prepare for the next step in problem solving.

Now it is time to analyze and organize the data collected. Help the children to focus continually on what their problem is so that they do not stray from it. With the problem clearly in mind, the children will start going through the slips of paper with the facts they have written down and make a judgment as to the relevance of each fact. If they find some which they feel are not important, they may put these away, but it is best not to *throw* them away at this point. Their next step is to group the slips which are left. Things can be grouped in many different ways. Help the children develop worthwhile criteria for their groupings. If the children are able, now is the time to have them generalize the information in each group. If part of their problem involves making an outline, these generalizations can help students develop outline headings.

During the next step—determining possible solutions—a more complicated thinking process is required of the students. Now they are going to apply the knowledge they have acquired to the problem, and see if they can solve it. The children will be asking themselves, Does this fact have any effect on the solution of the problem? What is the effect and what causes the effect? What are the similarities, the differences, the comparisons, the contrasts? During this process, the students are drawing from their bank of knowledge the facts that have any effect on this problem. At this point, children are attempting an overall generalization. Many students will need direction at this level.

The step of evaluating the solutions which appear to hold the most promise requires a value judgment. This is a high level of thinking, and one which every child will not be capable of; some may be able to take this step with guidance; others will do it automatically. Not all the children will be able to proceed to the final step without help, that is, applying the solutions they have discovered in some way.

When helping children with problem solving, think about the following hints: Be sure the children are ready for the step they are going to be asked to take; this will be the teacher's decision. Keep the first project relatively simple, and then keep a close watch on the progress so you can be there if the students run into trouble. Encourage children to think of all the resources that can be used. If the children overlook a few, come to their aid. Try to aim the project or problem at something that the children are really interested in, and if the children are going to work with a partner, help choose the partner they will benefit from working with. Sometimes it is helpful to pair a strong worker with a weaker one, but this should not be done all the time. Sometimes, in working with the students' objective, aides become so involved that they overlook their own objectives. Remember that just gathering the facts is not the goal of the team. Instead, the emphasis is upon the development of skills which enable the children to (1) locate information, (2) assess the material intelligently, and (3) apply it to a specific situation.

One excellent way a teacher has of helping children expand their thinking is to ask questions. The purpose of the questioning is much greater than checking to see if children know the correct answers. Questions can help children pull together information so that they see the relevance of it. Questions can open new areas of awareness, can stimulate an eagerness to continue the search for information, and can help children crystallize their values. To fulfill all these purposes, the questions asked need to be given a great deal of thought in relation to the desired result of the questions. Questions must have a real purpose. If the purpose is just to find out what the children know or what the children can recall, you may ask a rote question, such as: Who was the president of the United States during the Civil War? What is needed to turn water into steam? What is the name of the international group that works toward keeping peace in the world today? Questions of this kind require only that the children go back in their memory bank and pull out the answer that satisfies the question. Children do not have to apply other information, make inferences or value judgments. These questions often do have value. Through them you can discover which facts the child knows, and at what point you can begin working with the child.

If we want children to apply some of their knowledge and to see relationships, we need to ask them questions which will require them to compare or contrast ideas, understand sequential happenings, or think about cause and effect. Some questions of this type may be: Why did the Mormons settle where they did? Why do you think that this animal is found in desert regions? What are some factors people would have to think about before they could vote intelligently on this issue? This kind of questioning helps students to think over the information they have already accumulated and apply it to find new answers.

Sometimes we want children to think about what might happen if . . . ? These are called divergent questions, and the answers require both imagination and already acquired knowledge. Some examples of this kind of questioning are: What could be done if our fuel supply ran out? What changes might happen in our community if the freeway bypasses it? What would have happened to our country if it had been a Spanish ship with Spanish people who landed at Plymouth Rock? What would have happened if the *Mayflower* had landed in California? What can we do if our school is becoming littered? When children can try out their recommendations or speculations, they very often find out that they need to think further. For instance, the last question was actually put to a school student council. Their first answer was that trash receptacles should be placed on the campus. That was done, and the students found out quickly that it was not the complete answer. They had to think further to come up with a way to encourage students to put trash in the receptacles. Some of their ideas about how to do this worked. Some did not. The experience they derived from this, however, was worthwhile. Think of how important and how frequent this kind of questioning is. Workers in government, science, education, medicine, law, and many other professions use this type of questioning to solve their problems.

Another kind of question deals with values. These questions require students to evaluate or judge according to what they think is right. The following are examples of value questions: Should we have a dress code at school? Should the canyon be opened to builders? How could the check and balance system used in the United States government be changed to improve democracy, or should it be changed? Is the penalty for the possession of marijuana just? These are the kinds of question which adapt themselves well to a discussion group such as a panel or round table. They are not as valuable for a single report assignment. When we work with values, we are working with emotions, attitudes, feelings, and opinions. Children feel strongly that if they hear one side of a question, they should have the opportunity to give their side—and they should. More about values will be discussed later in this chapter.

In a question-answer or discussion situation, the teacher and aide need to be actively involved. They cannot sit back and mentally close off what is happening. They have to be ready with more questions which will stretch student's thinking even more. They cannot be content with one simple answer. This kind of answer is usually from students' recall level. Comments from the aide or teacher such as these will stimulate students to go beyond recall: What might happen next? What caused this to happen? What will the effect be? How would you feel if you . . . ? How would others feel? To help students organize their thinking and discussion, you might say, I don't quite understand you. Could you explain a little more?

Thinking is the most important skill that schools teach. Questions and discussions are strategies used to provoke thought. Teachers and aides need to develop those skills that help them know how, when, and who should be asked questions. This is not an inborn ability. Most of us are satisfied too quickly with one or two answers, and we do not probe further, taking the child as far as they can go in their thinking process. Much has been written about developing skills for clear thinking. For instance, Dr. William Glasser's book *Schools without Failure* introduces the class meeting. This is a dynamic tool for group discussions. You will learn leadership discussion skills from this book along with many positive ways of working with children.

Hilda Taba's books and classes on developing thinking skills are also effective. Ms. Taba's method stimulates and develops thinking through well-organized methods. Because the methods are so well ordered, most aides feel comfortable working with them after a short training period.

Many disciplines within the curriculum, especially science and the social sciences, are getting away from the grade-level subject-matter plan and are substituting a developmental spiral plan. The grade-level subject-matter plan presents certain units at certain grade levels. Transportation is studied in the third grade, electricity in the fifth grade, and algebra in the seventh grade. It is easy to see that there are advantages and disadvantages in this system. The advantages are in the areas of scheduling and arranging the curriculum. The disadvantages are that these divisions do not best account for the way children learn. For instance, many third graders are too young to grasp all the implications of transportation and apply these to the economy, westward expansion, and today's technology. Children are awed and excited by electricity long before the fifth grade. Many learning situations pertaining to algebra appear before the seventh grade. One of the big problems in a program structured according to grade level is that teachers are unable to make use of the most teachable moments. Another problem is that this plan does not consider how the children's thinking process is developing. Learning objectives do not build on each other in this structure. Not enough was known about the levels of thinking and the different kinds of thinking at the time that this system was widely applied in schools.

When Dr. Bloom and several associates working with achievement testing developed a way to organize and classify learning processes and arrange them in order from simple to complex, all existing systems began to seem less efficient. Dr. Bloom organized a taxonomy (or classification) of educational objectives in three areas of behavior:

1. The *cognitive,* which places the primary emphasis on the mental or intellectual process of learning.
2. The *affective,* which primarily emphasizes attitudes, emotions, and values of the learner, and is usually reflected by interests, appreciation, and adjustments.
3. The *psychomotor,* which places primary emphasis on physical skills.

The cognitive area is the one we are mainly concerned with in this chapter. Bloom and his associates classify the first level of learning as the recall or recognizing of facts. The next level is comprehension, which requires learners to interpret, or translate, and summarize the information they have received. Third is the level of application. For instance, once students learn percentages in their math class, they should then be able to figure the interest on their savings accounts. This level involves using the information in a situation different from the original learning situation. The next level is analysis, in which students analyze or separate a subject into parts, and draw comparisons and relationships between the elements. For instance, they may begin by comparing their weight on earth with what their weight would be on the moon. They may want to contrast industry during the Civil War with industry today. They may want to think about how a playground incident appeared to the playground supervisor, the principal, the custodian, the neighbors, and how different another child's view was from theirs. The fifth level is synthesis, which involves combining elements to form a new original thing, such as in producing a play, writing a story, practicing an art form, composing music, or inventing an object. The last level is evaluative, which is judging a thing based on a given set of criteria.[2] Can you see how closely question-answer skills are related to the thinking process?

Textbook authors and curriculum planners have used this taxonomy to revise subject content especially when and how subjects are presented to children. In the area of geography, for example, children learn in the primary grades that people live in different environments on the earth. Later, they learn that human beings change their environment to meet their needs. Still later, they learn that decisions which result from political, social, and economic issues also alter the environment. And so it is with each concept the child studies. This type of curriculum structure is known as the spiral plan, because it builds spirally on concepts already understood by the student.

Social Sciences

Are the social sciences, as some people claim, a fancy name for history and geography? Are they, as others suggest, a catchall category for anything that educators want to include in the curriculum but cannot find a justifiable place for? Fortunately, neither of these definitions is correct. In most school systems today, the social sciences are the study of people, their relation to each other and to the world around them. In the social sciences curriculum in the elementary school, information pertaining to human relationships is taken from history, geography, political science, economics, sociology, anthropology, science, and the humanities. This has not always been true.

Not too long ago each area of the social sciences curriculum, as we know it now, was treated as a separate subject, or not treated at all in the elementary school. A child might be studying American history and the geography of Asia at the same time. There was no attempt to make any relationships between the two. Educators began pointing out that studying the geography of the United States while learning about the history of the United States would make both

---

[2] *Paraphrased from* A Committee of College and University Examiners. *Taxonomy of Educational Objectives.* New York: David McKay Company, Inc., 1966, pp. 6–23.

Children learn about community and social problems. Here
children discover farming problems by caring for their own
garden.

areas more meaningful. The study of American economics and
American culture would also add meaning to all the other areas of
study because there is a direct relationship. Thus, it was concluded
that all these areas should be integrated as the curriculum of the
social sciences.

The logical sequence of the content in this curriculum seemed
to be to expand the study as the child's world expanded. This was
called the *widening horizon plan.* To be more exact, the study
would start with the family and the home, broaden out to the community, the state, the country, the world. It was logical, but it was
not psychologically sound. It was too rigid and uncompromising. A
child's interests and abilities are much more flexible than this. This
framework tended to lock in the curriculum. Topics become out-
dated rapidly, and this sequence does not allow for updating the
material. This plan dealt with human activities, but left the areas of
human concern untouched. The real problems of the world were
not being dealt with.

In most school systems today, social sciences include the study
of people, their relation to each other, and to the world around them.
Naturally, such a study is not going to be limited to history and
geography, but is going to include political science, economics, sociology, anthropology, science, and humanities. As you can understand, all these areas fit together and would lose their purpose and

effectiveness if taught separately. However, the kinds of knowledge to be dealt with are broad and, together, do not lend themselves to traditional methods of teaching. Out of this enlarged program content came changes in teaching techniques and strategies to include the problem-solving and thinking-development plan.

The opportunities for children to think and solve problems are everywhere. In the past, many teachers shut out these occasions by giving each child a book to read, and in many cases that book formed the outside limits of the child's world. Is there any wonder that some students left school firmly believing that the only cause of the Civil War was slavery, that many totally lacked understanding of the Indian's position during the westward movement of settlers, and that many were unaware that the Bill of Rights has any effect on our lives at the present time? A change was obviously needed.

Special projects may help children learn social sciences. For example, this aide is helping a group of children write a play about the early western movement.

The problem included knowing what changes needed to be made, how the teacher would work with these changes, and what new kind of organization would be used. The read-and-answer-questions method was out. So was studying isolated skills, such as map skills. Map skills, like most skills, are not important by themselves; these skills are important only as an instrument to help in solving problems and in seeing relationships. To help the teacher, social scientists revised their objectives and developed textbooks which presented the *spiral plan.* The teacher could then take the overall objective of the learning unit, break it down into learning goals, decide on the learning methods to be involved to reach these goals, determine who would be involved in working with these activities and the materials they would need, and then develop some kind of evaluation instrument to measure the students' learning.

The learning activities in such a new approach include many with which you are familiar. The activities include skills that are shared by other disciplines of the curriculum such as listening, speaking, reading, and writing. (We think of these as communication skills, so in this book they have been included in the chapter on communication. The chapter on communication also includes activities which are often used in the social sciences area, such as making reports, doing research, role playing, taking notes, developing outlines, etc.)

Map skills, chart and graph skills, and field trip procedures and suggestions will be included in this chapter, but they could also be useful in other disciplines of the curriculum such as math, science, creative arts, and reading.

Map Skills

Some of the map skills which will be integrated into the social sciences curriculum will begin in kindergarten and continue throughout the child's education. In kindergarten, children will talk about directions, up and down, front and back, left and right, and even north, east, west, and south. The children in kindergarten may draw their first map by drawing the classroom and putting in the furnishings. As they progress on through the grades, they may have the need to map the neighborhood or study a community map and then begin to use simple map symbols and a simple map key. The child progresses to being aware of the different kinds of maps, the meanings of parallels and their use, the simple scale, the understanding of projection and meridians. Some of the procedures which you may use to aid in the development of map learning throughout the elementary grades are:

1. Label directions on classroom walls.
2. Discuss the directions in which children are moving as they go on walks in and around the school.
3. Play games which involve using the right or left side of the body.

The children, with the help of the aide, have constructed a
map on the bulletin board. They will use this map during
their geography lessons.

4. Look at and discuss maps.
5. Study the apparent movement of the sun and earth.
6. Help children think about the earth's movement, about the poles and
    why they are so named. Be alert to the mistaken idea that children
    often have that north is up.
7. Experiment with devices which tell directions.
8. Help the children discover how directions may be given at night by
    locating the North Star.
9. Discuss events of common interest and find out where they happened.
10. Make comparisons between different maps.
11. Practice locating places which appear on maps.   ·
12. Notice traffic levels on different streets and roads.
13. Have students locate nearby railroad tracks, bus and truck routes, and
    air terminals.
14. Use every opportunity to refer to the model globe.
15. Let the children look at pictures which show different features in the
    landscape.

16. Listen carefully when children describe the location of things they are talking about.
17. Encourage students to use technical terminology.[3]

Most of these activities can be done informally as you visit with children on the playground, as they discuss a lesson with you, when you ride with them on a field trip, or as you are helping them choose a library book.

Other activities you may be involved with and which need more planning and organizing may be helping children to:

1. Draw maps.
2. Study the earth's rotation in relation to the sun and moon.
3. Construct globes to learn about the value of parallels and meridians in telling direction.
4. Make use of a variety of opportunities to measure distances.
5. Read books on map making.

If you, as the aide, are going to work with the children in map skills, you should know the meanings of the following terms:

Altitude	Mean solar day
Antarctic circle	Meridians
Arctic circle	Nautical mile
Circle of illumination	Orbit of the earth
Elevation	Parallels
Equator	Revolution of the earth
Equinox	Rotation of the earth
International date line	Sea level
Isobar	Solar day
Isotherm	Statute mile
Latitude	Tropic of cancer
Longitude	Tropic of capricorn[4]
Map projection	

You should also know the meanings of the following terms which are often used in geography:

Bay	Canal	Cape
Belt	Canyon	Channel

[3] From *Social Studies from Theory to Practice in Elementary Education* by Malcolm P. Douglas. J. B. Lippincott Company. Copyright © 1967, pp. 338–339.
[4] Ibid., p. 354.

Coastline	Isthmus	River system
Delta	Peninsula	Sea level
Dry lands	Plains	Strait
Gulf	Ravine	Stream
Harbor	Reef	Summit
Irrigation	River mouth	Tundra
Island	River source	Valley[5]

Reference materials such as an atlas, library books, films, film-strips, flat pictures, transparent globes, world maps, and outline maps are all helpful when working with maps.

You and the teacher may display maps or postcards showing geographical scenes, put up a large string of outline maps, or make a chart of geographical terms and relate them to a map.

The aide is selecting materials which children will use to learn map skills.

5   Ibid, p. 256.

The teacher may want the children to make their own maps. The following list suggests types of maps that children can make.

1. Use papier-mâché, sawdust mâché, salt and flour, powdered asbestos, or moistened sand to make relief maps. Large relief maps can be made on a section of the school yard or classroom.
2. Use chalk, tempera, and crayon on linoleum, paper, or oilcloth to make floor maps.
3. Use real samples of wheat, corn, cotton, and rocks to make specimen maps. Samples may be pasted on or exhibited in front of a large wall map with strings from object to place.
4. Use strips of paper for streets, pictures or silhouettes for buildings to make mural maps.
5. Make cellophane outline maps which show products, rainfall, and so forth. The cellophane maps can be placed over physical maps in order to show relationships.

The following directions for making relief maps should be helpful.

papier-mâché Tear into fine pieces 1½ sheets of newspaper. The paper should not be folded. Cover the paper with boiling water and stir until the mixture becomes a pulp. Mix two heaping tablespoons of flour with cold water. Add one cup of boiling water. Add the flour and water mixture to the paper pulp. One tablespoon of oil of wintergreen may be added to prevent souring. Model as with clay.

sawdust mâché Make paste of ½ pint of flour, one teaspoon of alum, one teaspoon of oil of cloves, and one quart of water. Cook flour and water to a creamy stage—add the alum just before removing the flour and water from the fire. Add oil of cloves immediately afterward. Stir in sawdust to a modeling consistency, adding dry sand, if needed. Paint with water paint and shellac.

salt and flour (an 18-inch map) Mix one cup of salt and one cup of flour. Pour in water gradually until dough is formed, which will drop from spoon but will not spread. Outline a map on cardboard and tack it to the solid surface. Mold detail on the outline and allow at least four days for drying; paint with tempera.

powdered asbestos (mixed with water) This is the best material to use because it is easily and quickly mixed, is inexpensive, can be used in small quantities, and can be added to easily. Both water color and tempera can be used on it. Allow for shrinkage.

A piece of plywood, the size needed for the map, should be used for the base. The outline of the map can be drawn on the board by standing it in the chalk tray and projecting the map on it with an opaque projector. Or the map can be traced from a large wall map. As they work, the children will need a large paper map of the same size as the relief on which the physical features are marked. Pictures help children visualize the topography of the country.

globe Inflate a playground ball or weather balloon. Choose one shaped like a globe. Cover the ball with waxed paper. Fasten the waxed paper securely with cellophane tape. Allow the opening of the ball to remain outside of the cellophane tape enclosure for later removal of ball. Cut 3-inch strips of newspaper. Wrap and paste several thicknesses of these strips all around and over the waxed paper. Allow each layer to dry before pasting another layer on the ball. Use your fingers to keep paper as smooth as possible. Use paper towels for the last coating. Allow paper to dry thoroughly. Cut slits in the globe at the opening of the ball so that the ball can be removed unharmed. Deflate the ball and pull it from within the new globe. Cover the paper-towel covering with blue calcimine paint. Cut the continents from paper and paste on outline drawn on globe. Shellac.

Graphs

Graphs, as a source of information for children, are very often overlooked, or left to the children to discover for themselves. When a child is studying mathematical concepts, such as percentages and fractions, some instruction in the use of graphs is presented; however, children should become acquainted with their use long before then.

Graphs designed for use in the social sciences are a combination of quantitative concepts and sociological information. The major types are pictorial, circle or pie shaped, area or solid, bar, line and curve. They are used to make comparisons of amount, position, time, value, length, height, temperature, volume, area, and related ideas and relationships. Their use must be in keeping with the child's level of development in quantitative thinking, mathematical concepts, and related experiences in social studies.

The most effective type of graph for elementary school children is the pictorial graph. Pictorial graphs can be made rather easily by securing pictures of the same size, assigning a unit value to them, and mounting them. To avoid confusion, pictures of uniform size must be used to compare such items as values of various farm and dairy products, or the relative speed of cars, trains, and planes.

There are certain skills involved in reading graphs that should be taught to children as they use them:

1. The child should survey the graph to determine the title or subject of the graph, the information presented, the size of the scales, and the symbols used to represent various items.
2. Facts should be read from the graph. For example, on a pie or circle graph, percentages can be read. On a line graph, quantities can be read by moving from a specific point on the line to the vertical and horizontal scales.
3. Interpretations can be made by comparing the different items presented, such as the speed of different means of transportation, the amount of production by states, or the sum of money spent for various purposes.
4. On some graphs, interpretations can be made in terms of growth trends or changes, for example, population, production, housing, and the like.[6]

An aide can help children understand graphs by showing them how to interpret the information on graphs whenever the child comes across a graph. Graphs may be found in their reading books, in resource books, and in many of their other textbooks.

The aide may also be called upon to construct graphs both for classroom use and for the teacher's own professional use.

Field Trips

One of the learning activities often used in the social sciences, but not limited in usefulness to that subject area, is the taking of field trips. Field trips contribute to learning in social studies. Concepts and understanding may be developed, extended, and clarified. Specific answers to questions may be secured. Students gain in-

---

[6] Michaelis, John U. *Social Studies for Children in a Democracy.* Englewood Cliffs, N.J.: Prentice-Hall, Inc., 2d ed. 1956, pp. 260–261.

creased appreciation of the relationship between the units being studied in school and the real world. Improved attitudes may result as children come face to face with persons and objects encountered on a field trip. Students learn to observe, record, question, and interview. Critical thinking is sharpened as children compare data gotten on field trips with material presented in texts. First-hand knowledge of social functions is gained as transportation, communications, production, conservation, and recreation are studied in operation.

The one significant difference between a field trip and just going somewhere is that a real educational purpose exists for the field trip. Careful planning is essential to assure learning. The actual planning is done by the teacher, the children, and the aide. Each has certain responsibilities. Attention is given to the following areas when planning is discussed: The purpose of the trip, ways to record information, safety precautions, time schedules, travel arrangements, wearing apparel, standards of behavior, and procedures to follow.

A field trip includes many small details which must be taken care of. Sometimes they seem almost insurmountable for the teacher. At times the teacher gives up the idea entirely because of the range of concerns and responsibilities involved. Many of these the aide can take over completely.

In most school districts many forms must be completed, such as requests for the field trip, parental approval forms, transportation forms, etc. Perhaps you can collect these forms and complete some of the items. When parental approval forms come back, collect and keep track of them. In some instances, a list of names, telephone numbers, and addresses of those children going on the trip is needed. You can supply this list. Question sheets may be typed, duplicated, and given to the children to help remind them of the information they are going to gather. The last few minutes before the trip begins require some checking on the part of the teacher and aide.

1. Does each child have a parental permission slip (if required)?
2. Does each child have a name tag?
3. Do you or the teacher have a roll sheet so you know exactly which children are with you?
4. If there were children who had to be left behind for any reason, are they taken care of?
5. Does each child appear well?

6. Is each child dressed according to the requirements of the trip?
7. Has each child had an opportunity to get a drink of water and go to the bathroom?
8. Have the rules for safety and behavior been reviewed?

During the field trip the teacher will need help with general supervision. The group should be kept together. All adults should be on the lookout for fatigue or disturbances and take precautionary steps. Before leaving the place visited, a check should be made to see that no one has left anything behind. The roll should be double-checked to be sure that no child was left behind. (The buddy system is helpful in this situation.) And thanks should be given to everyone who assisted with the field trip.

The destination of a walking or riding field trip represents only a fraction of what children can learn en route. Perception increases if children are prepared in advance to anticipate areas often unrelated to the trip itself—but nonetheless valuable. Here are some ideas of things that can be done en route with the children.

1. Read signs—store, street, road, advertising signs. Have the children try to spell what they see.
2. What geometric forms are visible in buildings and play areas? Draw designs on the chalkboard before the trip to coordinate art and math.
3. How many land formations do they find—hill, mountain, ravine, rocky area, sandbar, or island?
4. What does the color of the soil tell? (Red shows iron content, white indicates lime, black shows humus from decayed vegetable matter, and yellow indicates an impure iron content known as ocher, which is used in coloring paints.)
5. How many soil types can be observed—sand, gravel, silt, clay?
6. Look for signs of weathering or erosion in soil and rock. Did they see methods of conservation, reforestation, terracing, drainage, crop rotation, stripping, row crops, and grassland?
7. Look for water. Was it a brook, river, lake, waterfall, pool, puddle, well, ice, rain, or an ornamental fountain?
8. Observe shapes of trees, animals, leaves, shrubs, and flowers.
9. What colors can be seen?
10. Find manufactured and natural resources such as lumber, paper, pulpwood, cement, quarries, oil (observable wells), rubber, steel, etc.
11. Name and count animals.
12. Play animal, vegetable, or mineral.

13. Observe clouds. What distinguishes cumulus, cirrus, stratus, and nim-
    bostratus types? What weather do they indicate?
14. In what directions do the children travel to their destination? How many
    changes en route?
15. Estimate distance in blocks, miles, speed, and time.
16. Count bridges. Do they cross a highway, a railroad, or water? What
    types of bridges are they?
17. What kinds of work were people doing? Why? What tools or machines
    were they using?
18. What were children and adults doing for pleasure? Were they using
    any equipment?
19. What types of businesses and stores did they see? Why weren't they
    alike in size and location?
20. What sounds did they hear, what things did they feel, what smells did
    they smell?

Social sciences draw from and give to all other curriculum
areas. Many descriptions of the aide's tasks which have been discussed or explained in other chapters will also be pertinent to social
sciences. The tasks and ways of helping are many, and any alert
aide can find many places where help is needed. Many learning
experiences are available. The audiovisual materials, the resource
people, the construction activities, the field trips, the classroom
activities—all help to make the social sciences one of the most meaningful disciplines in the curriculum.

The aide must realize that one of the most important objectives
in the social sciences is the teaching and learning of values and attitudes. *Values* have been defined in many ways such as a standard, a
belief, a criterion for social behavior. Perhaps a meaningful and suc-
cinct definition is the following: Values of people are the rules by
which they live. The social sciences curriculum has not left the area
of values to be learned entirely outside of the school environment.
Values are a very important part within the social sciences curriculum itself, and should be an important part of the entire day's plan.

Many schools, in working with values, have turned to Laswell
and Kaplan's eight categories of values which they believe to be in
all open and free societies:

GENERAL VALUE TERM	SOME OF ITS INDICES
1. Affection	Love, friendship, congeniality, loyalty, emotional warmth, devotion, liking
2. Respect	Recognition, esteem, acceptance, reverence, worship, admiration, honor, consideration

3. Enlightenment — Understanding, insight, discernment, clarification (of meaning), generalization, discovery, knowledge (functional), wisdom

4. Skill — Talent (intellectual, social, communicative, physical, aesthetic), proficiency, craftsmanship

5. Power — Decision making, influence, control, restraint, rule, leadership, capacity to act, authority, sway, jurisdiction, command

6. Wealth — Economic security, goods and services, material culture, property, possessions

7. Well-being — Health (physical and mental), comfort, happiness, contentment, relative freedom from fear, physical and biological bases of adequacy

8. Rectitude — Moral, ethical, law-abiding, just, relative freedom from guilt, religious, responsible[7]

One way to work with children in values is first to provide experiences that will help them understand the value terms, and then integrate them into their own behavior. There are various methods of helping children recognize the different values. They may look through magazines, cut out pictures which illustrate a value, and identify which value the picture illustrates. (Sometimes there will be an overlapping of values.) You may also use role playing by having the children create situations where they can demonstrate the different values. Tell a story or show a film which has to do with values, stop the story or film in the middle, and ask the children to make up the ending of the story and, if they can, to identify the value they are using in their decisions. Show a study print or picture of a conflict situation, and then pose the students in the roles of the subjects of the picture. Ask the students to come alive when you snap your fingers and to dramatize how they dealt with the conflict. Maybe other students in the group would have dealt with the conflict in a different way. Let these students replay it or make suggestions.

A great deal of study has been done recently in the area of values. Already there are many materials on the market. There are

---

[7] Laswell, Harold, and Kaplan, Abraham. *Power and Society, a Framework for Political Inquiry.* New Haven: Yale University Press, 1950, p. 87.

textbooks, study prints, filmstrips, slides, films, recordings, bulletin board materials, and simulation games. However, if these are not available in your school, you still have a wealth of materials at hand. Take advantage of the happenings or situations in which your children are involved. Most of the time this is as meaningful as the commercial materials. Values become important to children when they touch their lives in some way. Sometimes teachers and aides are able to set up the situation; sometimes the situation is set up by circumstances, and we must be ready to make the most of it.

There are some important guidelines in working with children and values. Both the staff and the children need to be acquainted with the guidelines and to respect them.

1. Be ready to accept differences.
2. Listen to others before presenting your own view.
3. Be aware that facts are different from opinions.
4. Be open-minded and willing to change. (This is absolutely necessary in critical thinking.)
5. Be able to handle the subject objectively.
6. Don't moralize.

Be careful that no one is made uncomfortable. A child should not be embarrassed or made to feel frightened. This would be in direct opposition to the objective of teaching children about values.

It should be the aim of every school person to help young people learn to live by the values of democracy. The best way for children to learn this is for them to live and grow in a democratic environment. The classroom should be a place where individuals are respected, can make choices and decisions, assume and carry through responsibilities, use and help preserve rights, and have the opportunity to work with others toward common objectives. Concern for others, self-direction, critical thinking, cooperative group action, self-respect, acceptance of responsibility, and freedom of expression are necessary parts in democratic living. It is the responsibility of the school staff to see that the classroom environment is the kind which promotes and encourages these democratic values.

Science

Children live in a world informed by science, and that world is growing and changing constantly. Their present world causes them to ponder on the wonderments of it all. In their future, science will have an even more profound effect on them by changing their way of working and contributing to new ways of thinking. Science may help to develop a new way of life in which people are able to use new knowledge to solve basic social problems.

Children are naturally curious, imaginative, and anxious to find answers to help them understand their environment. They look to the school for help. This is a challenge that schools are accepting as they search for sound objectives which will give direction to the kinds of learning situations which develop in the classroom.

Children will be enthusiastic about science if they can experiment. Here an aide is helping a child put together a gasoline engine.

It is essential that schools first look at whom they are involving in their program. The range of students is a broad one, from children who will use science only in their everyday life to the boys and girls who will be medical specialists, electronic engineers, space technicians, or who will fill occupations which are as yet unknown. The school must present a science program to boys and girls who come from the country and from the city; to children who are world travelers and to children whose whole world is the city block they live on; to children who live with technological equipment daily and to those whose homes may still be without indoor plumbing. Can the schools provide a program for all? They can because schools no longer teach science as an accumulation of memorized facts. The new science programs, like the new social sciences programs, involve more than that. They involve skills, appreciations, understanding, and attitudes.

Science Conceptual Schemes

Who is to be taught has been identified. Now the question is, *What* will be taught? Everything in the world is in some way based on science. How does one organize it into a science curriculum? The National Science Teachers Association Committee on Curriculum Development suggests seven conceptual schemes. These schemes have been restated, reworded, and rearranged by authors, school districts, and state departments of education. The authors of *Concepts in Science* group the concepts this way:

1. When energy changes from one form to another the total amount of energy remains unchanged.

2. When matter changes from one form to another, the total amount of matter remains unchanged.

3. Living things are interdependent with one another and with their environment.

4. A living thing is the product of its heredity and environment.

5. Living things are in constant change.

6. The universe is in constant change.[8]

Each concept is brought up at each grade level, but not on the same level of complexity. Information, experience, and understanding increase as children grow more able to understand the complexity of these concepts. This, as you remember from the description in the social sciences portion of this chapter, is known as the spiral plan.

Now the question is, How are these concepts going to be presented to children who come to school with various backgrounds, interests, and abilities?

Before selecting the method that will be used to present the concept, the teacher will use some criteria as a basis for selecting

[8] Brandwein, Paul F., Cooper, Elizabeth K., Blackwood, Paul E., and Hone, Elizabeth B. *Concepts in Science.* New York: Harcourt, Brace and World, Inc., 1966, pp. 1–14.

appropriate learning experiences. The criteria may be:

1. Is the correct sequence used as it is related to the learners' maturity and as the concepts are related to each other?
2. Does it provide for the ability levels of the children to whom it is directed?
3. Is it based on problems which are related to the children's understanding?
4. Will it help the children develop critical thinking?
5. Will it aid children in developing favorable attitudes, and skills?
6. Will it develop skill in analyzing, appraising, and evaluating evidence before reaching decisions?
7. Will it encourage children to recognize the value of using many kinds of resources in solving problems?

The nature of science is such that it provides one of the most effective motivating forces to interest children. In the first place, science is all-encompassing. Ask children to look around the room and try to find one thing that isn't science-related in some way. They won't be able to, and that fact will impress them. Science is such a broad field that there has to be some parts of it that intrigue every child in the group. Maybe every child won't be inspired by the study of rocks, but some of the children will be fascinated by the study of plants. There are few children who are not excited by the study of animals and their behavior. Science, more than other subjects, encourages an organization of learning and thinking techniques. One learned fact pushes the student to learn the next, and the next, and on it goes. Also, since the facts are not static, they encourage more investigation. Science relates directly to children's lives, whether it be in direct relationship with their hobbies, their environment, their bodies, or whatever. With all these points in favor of science study, it is obvious that children will learn about science whether or not the schools do anything about it. What are some of the things we can do to help students learn even more than their natural curiosity prompts them to learn? How can we expand their interests and help them see relationships? Are there some things schools are doing that discourage children?

Let us first look at things we might be doing to make children dislike the study of science. It has been mentioned before that one teaching method used in teaching many subjects, and especially science, is the read-the-chapter-and-answer-the-questions-at-the-end method. This is an ineffective technique for most students in most curriculum areas, but it is even more frustrating in science. The book is providing the student with some exciting ideas and princi-

Using the science learning station prepared by the aide, this
teacher explains the principles of magnetism.

ples. At the same time, it is telling the children that science is an in-
vestigative study which should be experimented with and questioned. Scientists, children are told, have to prove their discoveries,
but when do children get to prove their discoveries? It doesn't
happen if the only activity in science is reading a book and answering the author's questions. What about the *students'* questions?

Another way children's spirit for science is broken is through
the rigidity of science programs, the sequence of science curriculum,
and the daily schedule. Many times children find things on their
way to school which they are excited about and are anxious to inves-
tigate. Their excitement and interest are destroyed if they are told
to put it away now, and we'll talk about it this afternoon at science
time, or that we are not studying about that this week. Take it home
and then bring it back next month when we are going to be studying
about it. These are teaching moments which need to be taken advantage of. It would take just a few minutes to talk about it and help
the child find the equipment needed for an investigation. Many
teachers take advantage of these moments by setting aside some time
at the beginning of the morning when students may share their find-
ings with their classmates. This is not to say that the science course
of study and the daily schedule should be thrown out, but some flexibility needs to be considered.

Children learn about the behavior of animals by observing
and caring for small animals which are kept in the classroom.

The behavior of living things can excite children when a variety
of animals is brought into the classroom, and the children are allowed time to observe and study their actions. Children learn much
about a kind of community living by watching ants work together in
an ant farm, or learn behavior by watching goldfish come to the surface for food when the food box is tapped on the edge of the
aquarium. A study of nutrition becomes more meaningful if the children have white rats to work with. Compare the knowledge that
might be gained in these situations with the learning that would take
place if the children just read that ants work together, that fish can be
trained to react to stimuli, or that rats and all living things need a bal-
anced diet.

If it is agreed that this discovery method is a more effective way
of learning, it makes you wonder why it isn't used universally. Of
course, the discovery method requires much preparation and a constant reorganizing and replenishing of materials. With so many
other pressures of the curriculum, teachers often do not have time to

The aide helps the child learn about electricity by helping
her assemble an electric circuit.

put this method into action. The capable aide is very often the element which makes this plan workable.

One of the important parts in the discovery program is providing a rich environment for the children to work in. This includes
bulletin boards, related books, related audiovisual materials, equipment and materials for experimentation, study sheets, or task cards.
All materials must be kept current, organized, and easily accessible.
Housekeeping is probably more needed in science than in other
fields both to set a good example for the children and for hygiene.
Let us look at some of the tasks which are connected with the
learning center if animals are there. Daily housekeeping of the pens
is essential. It is hoped that students would take this responsibility,
but they often need help from an adult. Special attention needs to

be given to expecting mother animals, nesting boxes must be available, and temperatures must be watched. If there are birds in the classroom, they must have proper exercise. Some animals are brought to school without proper homes. Most schools have cages available, but many times there is a problem of finding where the cages are, and once finding them, getting them ready for occupancy. Another problem with classroom animals is providing for their care during vacations. This is not to suggest that the aide should take all the animals home. However, finding homes for the animals might be part of the job. Sometimes, the children are required to take home written forms for their parents to sign, giving their approval of the children's keeping the animals. It also helps the parents if a note of suggestions for the care of the animal accompanies it. Sometimes this whole procedure can take several days, involve many notes and phone calls, and quite a bit of preparation of the animals and the cages.

Classroom pets must have proper care. This aide is teaching children how to care for and feed a newly born chick.

Plants also require attention, though not as much as animals. Containers are needed for them; they need food and water; they may need someone to care for them during the vacations. Many times terrariums need to be built, different types of soil need to be mixed so that growth and changes can be noted. One of the ideas in working with plants is to help children understand that all animal life depends on plants, that human beings, as creative as they are, are still not able to do what plants can do, make their own food. One important part of the study of plants is to study the various parts of them. An aide can set up experiments to provide opportunities for children to learn more about plants. For instance, a study of the root system might include putting some seeds on a wet blotter between two pieces of glass, so that children can watch the root system develop. Plant the seeds close to the glass in a terrarium, then put water at the other end of the terrarium. The students will see the roots grow toward the water. If you reverse the watering location, they will see the plant roots reverse their growing direction. To show the workings of the stem of the plant, place a celery stalk in a colored solution and watch the solution travel up through the cells to the leaves. To make this more dramatic, split the stalk into two or three sections and place each section into a different colored solution

Children learn about plants by caring for classroom plants.

and see the results. So much can be discovered about plants that every classroom should have many plants, and also someone to help care for them.

Good science teaching is enriched by the use of a variety of materials. Many of these materials are not wholly scientific materials, and therefore may be found in places other than the science closets. Teachers have complained that they dislike teaching science because it is such a chore getting together the materials for experiments. They realize that there is no substitute for firsthand experience and experimentation. They know that the children must have the opportunity to manipulate and observe things and events to really make the scientific method meaningful to them, but the fact remains that it takes much of the teacher's time and energy to collect the materials. When an aide collects, prepares, and stores materials, the teacher very often regains enthusiasm, and is able to develop a meaningful unit.

Some of the common things which are needed but seldom are where a teacher can get to them quickly are: candles, jars, wire, light bulbs, needles, pulleys, batteries, safety matches, string, medicine droppers, measuring spoons, flower pots, bags, boxes, blotters, plastic-foam forms, balloons, cellophane or plastic wrap, gummed labels, dowels, and glue.

Some of the tools which the teacher often needs but can seldom find are hammers, nails, tacks and screws, paints, tin shears, pliers, and tongs.

Some chemicals which are commonly called for are soda, starch, sugar, limewater, red ink, vinegar, table salt, paraffin, ammonia, powdered sulfur dyes, iodine, and yeast.

Collections which may be accumulated and used are seeds and fruits, leaves, shells, nests, rocks, fossils, and science pictures.

The audiovisual materials available for science are numerous and varied. Most science guidebooks include a list of the audiovisual materials which will correlate with the lessons. The aide can take the responsibility of ordering these materials and setting them up when the teacher is prepared to use them.

Every area in the study of science is rich with knowledge to be discovered and used. However, much attention is required from the classroom adults. Without this attention the whole program suffers. As an aide, you will find the science and social sciences areas exceptionally interesting to work in. And it won't take you long to realize how much the program is able to do when it has an adult team providing the experiences.

Chapter Summary

Social sciences and science are interrelated and dependent upon each other. They are more concerned with thinking and learning skills than they are with practice and drill. Emphasis in this chapter has been given to the development of the thinking skills but, in addition, includes materials, methods, and examples of learning experiences the aide should find useful.

social sciences Social science is the study of people and their relationship to each other and to the world around them. It is concerned with people and their interaction with the social and physical environment.

The social sciences deal with self-realization, human relationships, civic responsibility, and economic efficiency. Emphasis is placed on using knowledge and information to effectively solve meaningful life situations rather than on just learning and storing facts.

Social sciences include recognition and appreciation of world cultures, the uses of our natural resources and environment, the acceptance of responsibility for achieving democratic social actions, and all the various facets of our society that are utilized in achieving a balance between social stability and social change.

science The science curriculum in the elementary school is designed to give children a broad understanding of the physical world around them. Using scientific knowledge and taking advantage of the child's natural curiosity, skills are developed, and understanding is acquired in using scientific techniques.

Schools today teach children to participate in developments that take place in an ever changing world of science and technology. They learn to appreciate and understand their environment and to have a positive attitude toward it. The teaching methods used in science education emphasize the development of critical thinking.

Suggested References

A Committee of College and University Examiners. *Taxonomy of Educational Objectives.* New York: David McKay Company, Inc., 1966, pp. 6–23.

Barnes, Donald L., and Burgdorf, Arlene B. *New Approaches to Teaching Elementary Social Studies.* Minneapolis, Minnesota: Burgess Publishing Company, 1969.

Bloom, Benjamin S., Englehard, Max D., Furst, Edward J., Hill, Walker, and Krathwhol, David R. *Taxonomy of Educational Objectives.* New York: David McKay Company, Inc., 1956.

Booklet for Developing and Writing Performance and Process Objectives. Tucson, Arizona: Educational Innovators Press, 1970.

Brandwein, Paul F., Cooper, Elizabeth K., Blackwood, Paul E., and Hone, Elizabeth B. *Concepts in Science.* New York: Harcourt, Brace and World, Inc., 1966.

————, et al. *The Social Sciences, Concepts and Values.* New York: Harcourt, Brace and World, Inc., 1970.

Bruner, Jerome S., Goodnow, Jacqueline J., and Austin, George A. *A Study of Thinking.* New York: John Wiley and Sons, Inc., 1956.

Douglas, Malcolm P. *Social Studies from Theory to Practice in Elementary Education.* Philadelphia: J. B. Lippincott Company, 1967.

Jacobson, Willard J., and Tannenbaum, Harold E. *Modern Elementary School Science.* New York: Bureau of Publications, Teachers College, Columbia University, 1961.

Michaelis, John U. *Social Studies for Children in a Democracy.* Englewood Cliffs, N.J.: Prentice-Hall, Inc., 1956.

Sanders, Norris M. *Classroom Questions: What Kinds?* New York: Harper and Row, Publishers, Incorporated, 1966.

Science Dictionary, Discovering Natural Science. Chicago: Encyclopedia Brittanica, Inc., 1971.

Servey, Richard E. *Social Studies Instruction in the Elementary School.* San Francisco, Calif.: Chandler Publishing Company, 1967.

Silberman, Melvin L., Allender, Jerome S., and Yanoff, Jay M. (ed.). *The Psychology of Open Teaching and Learning Approach.* Boston: Little, Brown and Company, 1972.

Glasser, William. *Schools without Failure,* New York: Harper and Row, Publishers, Incorporated, 1969.

Taba, Hilda. *Curriculum Development: Theory and Practice.* New York: Harcourt, Brace and World, Inc., 1962.

————, and Hills, James L. *Teacher Handbook for Contra Costa Social Studies, Grades 1–6.* San Francisco: San Francisco State College, 1967.

Wagner, Guy, and Golloley, Laura. *Social Studies Games and Activities.* New York: Teachers Publishing Corporation, 1964.

Introduction

Elementary mathematics is usually not frightening to adults because they use it in their everyday activities. Most adults are secure in their ability to perform the four standard operations (addition, subtraction, multiplication, and division), to use measurements, to work with fractions, and some are even confident in their use of geometry and algebra. However, when a school announces that it is going to teach *new math,* teachers tremble, parents panic, and teacher aides find another occupation. This description may be somewhat exaggerated, but many teachers, parents, and aides express great resistance to *new math* programs. The children who are working in new math programs, on the other hand, are often enthusiastic about the program. Their spontaneous comments frequently are: Oh, I get it now! Now I understand it! Oh yeah, now that makes sense! Is math over already? Let's not have the assembly during math time!

Perhaps many adults reacted to the term *new math.* Most people had the feeling that math was a static science. They were familiar with time-honored methods of teaching and using math. Changes in methods of teaching reading, in the social sciences curriculum, in approaches to other sciences, and in ways of improving physical education skills were all taken in stride by the public. However, when the math curriculum was "tampered" with, everyone's security was shaken. It need not be true. Learning new math can be fun and is a rewarding experience. You will be amazed at how many times you say, Oh, now I see why I have been doing that certain thing all these years!

The Why of New Math

New math shifts the emphasis from teaching mathematics as a way of doing something to teaching it as a way of thinking. The major emphasis is therefore placed on the understanding of basic mathematical concepts which may be hidden within computational techniques. Certainly computation is an important part of math and must be taught, but not until the child understands the underlying mathematical concepts.

The responsibility of the classroom teacher and the aide is to help children understand the number system so that the children can use the correct processes in appropriate situations, and so that the children will be aware of the number problems con-

1 2 3 4 5 6 7 8 9 10

mathematics 4

tained in various situations. They will then understand when quantitative thinking is required. The ability to do arithmetic operations and the ability to apply the correct mathematical processes are the two main objectives in the modern school mathematics curriculum.

These two objectives have been regarded by some as involving mathematical aims and social aims. It is not a case of choosing between the mathematical aim and the social aim. Instead both aims are reached through the arithmetic program.

Some basic math concepts can be taught with money. Here a child learns counting by using a chart prepared by an aide.

Arithmetic classes are structured in different ways. In some classrooms the teacher presents the concept to the whole class. And in some of these situations the whole class is expected to move at the same pace, cover the same material, grasp the same concepts. In other situations, the teacher presents the same concept to the entire class but develops the concept differently with different children. For instance, the slower math students will work with the concept on a very concrete basis; the average student will work with the concepts on a semiconcrete basis; and the faster students will go quickly from the concrete to the abstract. Some classrooms are set up with permanent math groups working at different levels. Some classrooms are organized on an individual basis where each child works at his or her own speed in a textbook or a kit. When a new concept is approached, the student has an individual conference with the instructor who explains it. Then the child becomes involved in learning experiences to reinforce this concept. Later, the child and the teacher evaluate the child's understanding, after which the child begins the next concept.

Children can learn math at their own speed. This child is getting help from an older student in filling out a math task card.

The traditional math program tended to build great strength in math through drills, but the ability to analyze problem situations was not particularly well developed. One day in the math class was very much like every other day. There were three steps to presenting new material. The teacher explained the concept, the children worked a few problems under the teacher's close supervision, and then the assignments were made. The brighter students in math did the same problems as the slower students, but did more of them.

Today, teachers recognize the many factors involved in guiding a child's learning in arithmetic. They realize that in some situations drill is necessary, but that an arithmetic program which includes only drill will not prepare children to solve the quantitative problems they encounter. Therefore, it is necessary to provide learning experiences for children so that they can analyze problem situations independently. These experiences include experimenting with numbers, asking questions, and thinking through mathematical situations. The arithmetic program should contain many activities that will help children obtain greater skill and understanding of the abstraction found in numbers.

The modern arithmetic program requires the help of the teacher aide much more than the traditional program does. The modern pro-

Programmed math assignments are designed so children can learn at their own rate. The aide helps these boys work on programmed materials while other children use teaching machines.

gram attempts to relate arithmetic experiences to the child's real-life situations. Children are permitted enough freedom to recognize, study, and attack number problems according to their individual needs. The teacher's position of leadership, planning, guiding, and assisting becomes broader and more important. The teacher is concerned with the implications of the child's learning processes, the child's needs and interests, and the demands of society on the child. This is a big responsibility for one person, almost an impossible one to carry out satisfactorily. However, with a team of teacher and aide, the program can progress smoothly and effectively.

To make this team work, the aide needs to understand the total math program; to know the new math methods, the vocabulary, and the concrete aids that are available, and to know how to use them; and to be able to recognize situations within the child's school day that will help reinforce mathematical learning. Most aides will not be able to depend completely on their own experiences in math classes. The program has changed since most of them were involved in elementary school math, so they are going to have to get their background some other way. There are many opportunities. The school's professional library will contain books on new math. Many of our professional teacher magazines include articles about new math and give many good ideas to use in the classroom. Bookstores sell materials to help parents work with their children in new math. School districts often hold workshops for the teachers in new math, and some districts also invite their aides to attend. Many colleges offer courses in new math so the opportunities to get help in this subject area are many.

When new math shifted the emphasis from teaching math as a way of doing something to teaching it as a way of thinking and understanding, certain other changes were bound to happen. Methods, materials, objectives, and sequence changed. In the following pages, some of the main concepts will be introduced and explained; the more commonly used new math terms will be defined; math materials to develop certain concepts will be included; and some math games will be given to help you begin your instructional game collection. With this background, an aid should be able to take on duties in the classroom. It would not be fair to the aide or to the student if the aide were not cautioned against making off-the-cuff explanations. Either ask the teacher for help when you are questioned in an area that you are not sure of or use the teacher's guide to the math text to help you.

Math Theories

sets One of the most fruitful ideas from a mathematical, as well as an educational, point of view has been the development of the concept of *set*. Counting and numbers are abstract notions, and they must be developed patiently and carefully. Children need to see and handle many collections of two things before they are aware of the common property which is called *twoness*. These things may be beads, beans, sticks, buttons, pencils, crayons—any concrete things which encourage children to discover patterns and relations. As the children work with these groups of objects, the first mathematical ideas are initiated.

If you ask a child, What is a set? the child will probably answer that it is a group of objects, and the objects contained in that group are called elements or the members of the set. Other expressions for a set may include *team, class, troop, club*. They all mean any collection or group of things. Any set can be described in terms of a condition which is satisfied by all the elements of the set and by nothing else, such as *a set of red pencils.* The condition of being red determines the set. A black pencil would not belong to this set. Sometimes sets are described by words, such as "all the states in the nation west of the Rocky Mountains." Sometimes pictures of sets are used to help us communicate both the idea of a set and a description of its elements.

Whatever the elements of the set are, they are placed within braces. For instance, the symbol $\{0, 1, 2, 3, 4, 5\}$ is simply a name for the set described by the phrase, "the set of whole numbers from zero through five." Sometimes it is convenient to use a capital letter as a temporary name for a set. The statement $A = \{0, 1, 2, 3, 4, 5\}$ is read "A is the set of whole numbers from zero through five." In some cases, the set will not contain any members. For example, a set of all the original thirteen colonies west of the Mississippi River; clearly, there are no members to this set, so it is called an empty set, and its symbol is $\{ \}$ or $\emptyset$.

A *subset* of a set contains members of the original set. An illustration of a subset might be

Set:	$A = \{1, 2, 3, 4, 5\}$
Subset:	$B = \{2, 4\}$

You see that every member of B is also a member of A, therefore B is a subset of A. Every member alone, or in combination with another member, is a subset of set A. (Empty sets and the full set are also subsets of the parent set.)

The sets of elements which are common to each of two sets is called the *intersection* of the two sets. For example

$$\text{Set } A = \{\text{Mary, Paul, Jim, Ann}\}$$
$$\text{Set } B = \{\text{John, Paul, Sally, Ann}\}$$

You see that Paul and Ann are in both sets, so the intersection of set A and set B gives us a new set, which we will call set C, and which is the *intersecting* set, so

$$\text{Set } C = \{\text{Paul, Ann}\}$$

The intersecting symbol is $\cap$. $A \cap B = C$.

The *union* of two sets such as sets A and B is a set consisting of all the members of set A and all the members of set B. The symbol for *union* is $\cup$. For example, set $A = \{a, b, c, d, e,\}$; set $B = \{e, f, g, h,$

i}. When we make a union of the two sets, we say

$$A \cup B = C, C = \{a, b, c, d, e, f, g, h, i\}$$

It is not necessary to write *e* twice.

systems and numeration   Any word or symbol which is used to name a number is called a numeral. Systems of writing numerals are called systems of numeration. Numeration systems include tally marks, Egyptian numeration symbols, Roman numerals, and the Hindu-Arabic system of numeration which we use as does most of the world. There are ten basic symbols in our system of numeration:

$$0, 1, 2, 3, 4, 5, 6, 7, 8, 9$$

These symbols are called digits. The place of a digit in a numeral is extremely important. If the position is changed, its value is changed. The place value principle of the Hindu-Arabic system of numeration may be shown this way:

. . .	Ten thousands	Thousands	Hundreds	Tens	Ones
		2	7	3	1

Because our system of expressing numbers uses the principle of grouping by tens, it is called a *base ten system* of numeration. It is also known as a decimal system (from the Latin word *decem*, meaning ten). It is believed that the choice of ten as a base for the numeration system stems from the fact that human beings have ten fingers for counting. However, some civilizations have used bases other than ten, and, in some situations, we do so now. Seconds and minutes work on a base 60; inches work on a base 12.

Let us pretend we are on a base 5 or a quinary system. Now, five symbols are needed, so 0, 1, 2, 3, and 4 will be used. When we have a value of 8 in base 10, we would have 13 in base 5. (8 = 1 five and 3 ones.)

The use of other number systems will take practice, and so allow some time to work with this concept yourself before you begin helping children, or you will not only frustrate yourself, but you will confuse the children. They are able to think in other bases much easier than we, who are base 10 oriented and have been for years. However, when their adult helper does not know for sure what way to go, their confidence may be shaken.

open sentence and solution sets   To communicate ideas, mathematical or otherwise, we use sentences such as: The pencil is short.   California is west of Ohio.   Proper nouns have capital letters. 7 + 4 = 11.   Hitler was the ruler of Russia.   All these sentences make definite assertions.   Some assertions are true; others are false.   In mathematics, a sentence that may be judged true *or* false is called a *statement*.   In mathematics, statements of equality and statements of inequality are common.   Statements such as

$$6 + 4 = 10$$
$$2 + 2 + 2 + 2 = 8$$
$$9 \div 5 = 4$$
$$3 \times 4 = 12$$
$$36 \div 6 = 6$$

are all statements of equality.   Whether true or false they are called equations.   Statements of inequality are shown this way: $6 + 4 \neq 11$. The symbol $\neq$ means *is not equal to.*

Statements of inequality involving numbers are often given using the notions of *greater than* and *less than*.   The symbol for *greater than* is $>$, and the symbol for *less than* is $<$.   Thus we have $5 > 4$ and $2 < 3$.

A number line is quite useful in determining the truth value of statements of inequality.   The numbers on the line are arranged in order of increasing value from left to right: 0 1 2 3 4 5 6 7 .

An open sentence implies that a certain place in the sentence has been left open but is meant to be filled by making a proper choice.   For instance: _____ was the first president of the United States.   This open sentence is neither true nor false, and will become meaningful only when the blank is filled in.   In elementary mathematics, you might encounter an open sentence such as _____ + 5 = 10.   Perhaps, rather than using a blank, a frame may be used, so the sentence will be written $\square + 5 = 10$.   A mathematician prefers to use a letter called a *variable*, instead of a frame or a blank, so he or she would write the sentence $x + 5 = 10$, the choice of the letter being arbitrary.

structure   One satisfying aspect of mathematics is that math contains patterns, and, as students, we search for these patterns and determine the conditions under which such patterns hold.   When we see a certain result happening over and over again, we tend to think that with the same conditions this result will always happen.   This is called *inductive* reasoning.   However, structure and *deductive* reasoning, which is the process of coming to a conclusion from a principle previously established, is central to the growth of all mathematical studies. Modern mathematicians emphasize the mathematical method. Start with a set of statements whose truth we agree to accept, and then use deductive reasoning to build the remainder of the mathematical structure. In order to understand new mathematics, it is necessary to understand both the nature and the role of deduction in math, in addition to the significance of the mathematical method. The basic ideas or building blocks are presented here with the definition of the idea and some types of examples.

The operations of addition and multiplication have a *commutative law*. The assumption of this law is that the sum or the product of two numbers is the same regardless of the order in which you add or multiply them. In other words, $4 + 5 = 5 + 4$, or $3 \times 7 = 7 \times 3$. The commutative law does not apply to subtraction or division because $7 - 4 \neq 4 - 7$ and $21 \div 7 \neq 7 \div 21$.

The *associative law* applies to addition and multiplication. In mathematics we use the binary operation, that is, we work with two numbers at a time. For instance, if we want to add more than two numbers, we add in groups of two. This can be done in several ways. For example, consider the following problem: $2 + 4 + 6$.

$$2 + (4 + 6) = 2 + 10 \qquad \text{or} \qquad (2 + 4) + 6 = 6 + 6$$
$$= 12 \qquad\qquad\qquad\qquad\qquad = 12$$

As shown, both interpretations lead to the same result.

Together, the commutative and associative laws for addition make it possible to add a set of numbers in any way. Similarly, together, the commutative and associative laws for multiplication enable us to multiply a set of numbers in any way.

The *distributive law* states that the product of a number and the sum of two numbers are the same as the sum of the products obtained by multiplying each of the other numbers by the first number. For example, consider the following problem: $2 (4 + 6)$. Because of the distributive law, this problem can be solved in either one of two ways:

$$2(4 + 6) = (2 \times 4) + (2 \times 6)$$
$$2(10) = 8 + 12$$
$$20 = 20$$

Multiplication is distributive with respect to addition.

The distributive law may be expanded over any two operations which are not inverses of each other. Thus, it may link multiplication to either addition or subtraction. It also may link division to either addition or subtraction. However, it may not link addition to its inverse, subtraction, nor may it link multiplication to its inverse, division.

The preceding pages have provided a brief glimpse of some of the new approaches in mathematics and have attempted to explore some of the basic concepts. Obviously, this is just to provide you with a starting point in new math. Your next step should be to enroll in a math class or to obtain a guidebook and solve the problems as the procedure is explained to you.

The role of the aide in the math class is simply to help students when help is needed. This, of course, is the obvious reason for having the aide in the classroom in general. However, the ways in which an aide helps are varied.

One successful method of helping students has been compared to the doctor-nurse-patient setup. A group of students who have the same need gather into one area. The need may be that the group is prepared to learn a new concept. The teacher moves into the group and presents the concept, quickly checks to see if the students understand the idea, and then moves on to another group with a different need. As the teacher moves away from a group, the aide moves in to carry out the prescription the teacher has given, which may involve doing a work sheet, viewing a filmstrip, or reading a book. The aide's role is to reinforce the teaching that has been done by the teacher. When the students are able to work independently, the aide moves on to the next group where the teacher has just finished presenting the lesson.

Sometimes aides are assigned to take care of the drill work. They may use flash cards, learning games, or worksheets with a

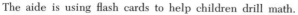
The aide is using flash cards to help children drill math.

group. Aides will occasionally accompany children onto the playground or take them into other areas of the school to solve a practical problem such as measuring the baseball diamond, finding angles, or counting particular items.

New math makes use of many materials other than the math book. Some of these materials can be made by the aides, some can be supplemented by the aides. In other cases, children need an aide with them to use these materials effectively. The teaching aid chart and the ideas which can be developed from it are included here.

Children learn how to measure by checking and recording plant growth.

Teaching Aid	Ideas Which Can Be Developed	
Countingframe	One-to-one matching	Place values
	Ordinal numbers	Renaming numbers
Flannel board	Cardinal numbers	Associative law
and objects	Ordinal numbers	Renaming
	One-to-one matching	Identity elements
	Equivalent sets	Geometric shapes
	Nonequivalent sets	One more, one less

Teaching Aid (Continued)	Ideas Which Can Be Developed (Continued)	
Flannel board and objects	Equal sets Greater than, less than Addition, subtraction Commutative law	Inverse relations Fractional parts Equations
Peg board and pegs	Cardinal numbers Ordinal numbers Addition, subtraction Renaming numbers Skip counting Commutative law Greater than, less than	Associative law Inverse relations Equivalence, nonequivalence Equality of sets One more, one less Geometric shapes
Blocks	Addition, subtraction combinations through eight	One more, one less Fractional parts
Picture cards	Cardinal numbers Matching with numeral and number name	Equivalence Nonequivalence
Numeral cards	Cardinal numbers Ordinal numbers Addition, subtraction Renaming numbers	Commutative law More than, less than Equations
Word cards	Addition, subtraction Equations	Matching with numerals and picture cards
Expanded notation cards	Place value	Renaming numbers
Number line	Cardinal numbers Ordinal numbers Commutative law	Associative law Skip counting
Addition chart	Addition facts Seeing patterns Ordinal numbers	Identity elements Commutative law
Ten frame	One more, one less Commutative law	Renaming numbers Addition, subtraction
Cuisenaire rods	Addition, subtraction	Commutative law

Teaching Aid (Continued)	Ideas Which Can Be Developed (Continued)	
Cuisenaire rods	Multiplication, division	Associative law
	Ratio, proportion	More than, less than
	Fractions	Inverse relations
Geo-board	Geometry	Finding area
	Set theory	

Organizing Math Activities

Games and other activities are a large part of learning elementary mathematics. Some of these can be bought, and many are made by the staff. It not only takes a great deal of time to make the games, but it also takes time to introduce them to the children. Both jobs are often assignments given to aides. Some games will have to be made by the aides because they are fairly complex and require skill; but there are other games the children can help make. Often, children learn by constructing the game.

Children can learn to add, subtract, and count by using the ten frame.

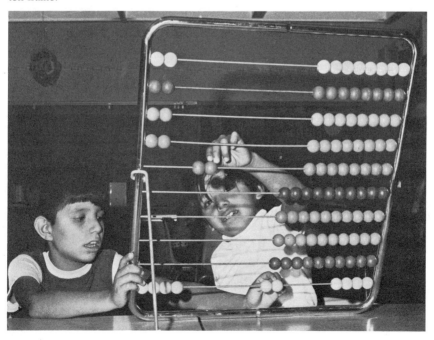

Some schools have a group of parents who are volunteer help-
ers and who are willing to help in the classroom. Although effective
help for the children often requires more training and time than volunteer parents have, they are helpful in game-making tasks if a time
schedule can be satisfactorily worked out. Parents need some direction in making themselves useful in these situations, and the teacher
aide is often the best qualified person to give this direction. With an
aide and parent-volunteer more games might be made for use in the
classrooms, and parents would discover a great deal about the capable and efficient work of both teachers and aides.

These children are using Cuisenaire rods to learn principles of arithmetic.

Examples of Math Activities

set booklets Have children prepare their own set booklets
from groups of pictures cut from magazines. For instance, they can
develop equations showing three girls plus five boys equal eight
children. In this way they begin to see a relationship between
numbers and reality. Such an activity, related to real-life situations,
gives children a greater appreciation of math processes.

geometric collages Begin by drawing a large circle, square, triangle, and rectangle on the chalkboard. How many forms can the children identify? Ask them to tell you how to make the same figure larger and smaller. Discuss the shapes. What can they see in the classroom that is the same as any one of the shapes? The flag for the rectangle? A phonograph record for the circle? What happens when they divide each geometric shape by drawing a line through the center? What new shapes do they see? Then let the children get busy with colored construction paper, scissors, pencils, and rulers to duplicate the shapes on the board in a variety of sizes.

Start the actual collage by suggesting that children choose and move pieces until they begin to see a chicken, clown, or dog emerge. For instance, does the square suggest a body, the circle a head, and the rectangle an arm or a leg? How can they make buttons, feet, eyes, and a mouth?

In the process of creating, children soon discover that the size of a shape alters the effect by making something more realistic or humorous. Have the children assemble and paste their chosen shapes on large sheets of construction paper. Let them talk with each other about the new shapes they created in making the collage.

doughnuts Make a large tagboard doughnut about 24 inches in diameter. Cut out the center. Around the outside edge, print numbers from 1 to 10. Hang it on the chalkboard. In the center on the chalkboard, write 5. A child must then add 5 to each number on the doughnut, putting the answer outside the rim on the chalkboard. After checking the answers, change the number in the center and have another child work the problems. This is good for all four basic math operations.

These are a few examples of math activities. Many more can be found in math books, in teachers' magazines, or picked up in conversations with teachers. One very practical way of keeping track of math games is to write the directions for each game on separate index cards. File these under headings such as *sets, measurements, bases, addition, subtraction, fractions,* etc. When you are assigned to work with a group in one of these areas, you can quickly go through that group of cards and pull some that would be appropriate for the lesson. You may also want to build a collection of games which can be used at the math centers. When you are thinking about games for the math centers, don't overlook the old favorites which all children love, such as chess, Monopoly, Life, dominoes, to name just a few.

Children can learn many math concepts through games. For example, by hanging weights on a balance, children learn the principles of addition.

Chapter Summary

Grade school mathematics has changed considerably in recent years. Those who learned math under the old system are confused by terms such as *sets, subsets, base 3,* etc. Many adults wonder why educators seem to have made math even more confusing. The fact of the matter is that the opposite may be true. Many children now find math more interesting and meaningful. The reason for this is that the emphasis in new math is placed on *understanding* basic mathematics ideas rather than solving problems using an unexplained rule or formula. New math still requires computational skills to execute the operations or processes of arithmetic. Children must be aware of numbers in their daily lives so that they may use the proper arithmetic operations in solving problems. They must also learn to analyze problem situations and to be able to solve quantitative problems.

An effective new math program requires the cooperation of the teacher aide to a much greater degree than the traditional program does. Children are given more freedom to recognize, study, and attack problems. They will develop problem-solving skills as quickly or as slowly as their own abilities allow. Therefore the new math program is more individualized than the traditional programs. It is difficult for the teacher to effectively handle even an average-sized class on an individual basis. Thus the teacher aide who has been trained in this area can almost double the efficiency of the teacher.

Suggested References

Adler, Irving. *The Giant Golden Book of Mathematics: Exploring the World of Numbers and Space.* New York: Golden Press, Inc., 1960.

Biggs, E., and MacLean, J. *Freedom to Learn: An Active Learning Approach to Mathematics.* Reading, Mass.: Addison-Wesley Publishing Company, Inc., 1972.

Corle, Clyde G. *Building Arithmetic Skills with Games.* Dansville, New York: The Instructor (pamphlet), 1968.

Gundlach, Bernard H. *Student's Glossary of Arithmetical-Mathematical Terms.* Sacramento: California State Department of Education, 1964.

Haugaard, James C. and Horlock, David W. *Fun and Games with Mathematics.* Los Gatos, California: Contemporary Ideas, 1972.

Heimer, Ralph T., and Newman, Miriam S. *The New Mathematics for Parents.* New York: Holt, Rinehart and Winston, Inc., 1965.

Lawson, Ernestine M. *Introducing Children to Math.* Dansville, New York: The Instructor (pamphlet), 1970.

Nichols and Swain. *Mathematics for the Elementary School Teacher.* New York: Holt, Rinehart and Winston, 1971.

Weaver, Jay D., and Wolfe, Charles T. *Modern Mathematics for Elementary Teachers.* International Textbook, 1968.

Introduction

This chapter could have been entitled "Art and Music." However, the discussion of music and art in this chapter is a way of discussing the larger topic of creativity in children and ways to encourage it. Art and music are easy springboards for the teacher, teacher aide, and the children to many kinds of creative participation.

According to some definitions, creativity is a kind of *divergent* thinking: many answers are possible. In a process of *convergent* thinking, only one answer is correct. When we think of various school programs, we see that many, perhaps most, tend toward developing convergent thinking. Teachers tend to ask one-answer questions and show disapproval if an unexpected solution is offered. However, schools are beginning to realize that in a complex society we are faced with a growing number of problems which require divergent thinking. Therefore recent teaching methods emphasize investigating, experimenting, problem solving, and creative undertakings. It is easy, then, to understand how creativity is a part of the entire school curriculum.

We know that everyone is born with certain creative abilities. So it becomes an obligation of the schools to provide situations and environments where this creativeness can flourish and grow. Classroom teachers and aides have the task of providing situations and an environment which help develop creativity in the everyday life of the child. It is essential that the setting for creative work be provided for the children. Such settings will include:

1. An open, friendly classroom atmosphere.
2. Emotional competition replaced by acceptance, both by the children and by the adult leaders—an atmosphere which encourages divergent thinking.
3. Opportunity and encouragement for creative expression throughout the school day, not just one or two hours a week.

The last point needs to be emphasized. If schools accept the fact that creative activity in art, music, and drama is important for the overall development of the child, then it follows that creative activity is necessary throughout the day and throughout the week. Creativity will extend to other areas of the curriculum and schedule if permitted. This does not mean, however, that creativity is to be encouraged at the expense of a scheduled lesson or the development of skills. Carefully planned experi-

creative arts

ences which help to develop skills in art, music, drama, etc., must be included in the education of the child. The creative aspects, however, cannot be scheduled. Creativity will occur spontaneously in a suitable atmosphere. Creativity in all areas of the curriculum must be a continuing concern of school personnel.

Music

Music is a creative means of communication. Children get much satisfaction out of singing and playing, writing songs and music, listening to recordings or performing, reading music and moving to music. Each of these activities provides an outlet for creative drive.

Small children love to sing and will do so with the slightest encouragement. This enthusiasm will continue with older children if the music selected appeals to them, and if the situation is enjoyable. If you work with children in their music programs, you will find certain simple unison songs which can be learned by ear that will encourage free and happy singing. Children will also find part singing an enriching experience, but it usually is not started until the middle grades. Sometimes instruments take one part of the music while the voices carry the other part. If instruments are not easily available, the children can make many kinds. This is a wonderful opportunity for them to experiment with sounds. While using instruments, the children will become aware that there are three different types: *rhythm, melody,* and *chording* instruments. Using these instruments will help children to understand the voices of the orchestra and will lead to better listening.

Children enjoy the following musical activities:

LEARNING TO SING
1. Songs about home and school
2. Songs about people, especially songs in which children can substitute their own name or a friend's name
3. Songs with special phrases, such as catchy nonsense words or repeated phrases
4. Songs involving action—clapping, hopping
5. Songs the children themselves make up about their daily activities
6. Popular songs that they hear on television, radio, or movies
7. Songs that are appropriate for seasons of the year or holidays
8. Songs that children can dramatize
9. Catchy musical commercials

LEARNING TO PLAY

1. Drums
2. Bells
3. Rhythm sticks
4. Sand blocks
5. Shakers
6. Cymbals
7. Mouth organs
8. Ocarina
9. Simple musical instruments
10. Water-filled glasses
11. Autoharp
12. Piano

Some children really enjoy writing music or putting some of their writing to music that is familiar to them. To help them do this, the teacher and teacher aide will find a general knowledge of music helpful. The musical scale is the place to start with the children. When the child is familiar with the music scale, then you can discuss whether the notes are the same, higher, or lower, or whether there is one step or more than one step. You can discuss how the loudness or softness of the selection helps to set the mood whether it is the same as the movement of the music, or whether it is faster or slower. A repetition of a musical phrase has its effect on the musical message. So does a steady rhythm.

While the aide plays a piano, these children learn a new song.

Young people thoroughly enjoy extemporizing by singing with the accompaniment of guitar or Autoharp. If this is done with a group of children, each may contribute an original verse. It is not necessary that the song be written down for the children to have the satisfying experience of creating and communicating through music. Music can be enjoyed in all areas of the school program. In a social sciences unit, for example, the children will enjoy writing music to go with a particular period of history or with the topic they are studying.

Listening is an important part of musical activities. Children are better able to sing, play instruments, and respond to music in rhythmical movement when they have developed the habit of listening intently. There are certain things to listen for, such as:

1. The tempo and the beat of the music
2. The dynamics (loud or soft) of the selection
3. The phrasing of the melody
4. The shape of the melody
5. The mood of the music and what instruments help set this mood
6. The harmony

Of course, children cannot listen for all these effects at one time. One should be selected and emphasized at a time. Children should also have time for quiet listening to music, simply to enjoy its beauty. This may be enhanced by such aids as pictures, poetry, and stories. Live music is also a desirable activity for the children. Perhaps a classmate, or an older student, or a community musician will visit the classroom and perform for the children. Additional listening activities include listening to learn a new song, listening carefully in order to put a story to music, and listening to provide motivation for creative writing.

Many classrooms have a music center set up for the children to explore on their own. It usually contains a record and/or tape player and earphones along with a variety of records and tapes. Some of these will set a mood for the listening child, some will comfort a frustrated one, and some will help the child identify the instruments of the orchestra.

Music, as we mentioned before, is helpful in all curriculum areas. Music plays an important part in the building of understanding in the social sciences area. The torment of the slaves is revealed through Negro spirituals, the triumphant exultation of people at Easter and Christmas time is reflected in Easter and Christmas music. The spirited mood of march music inspires patriotism, and gay Mexican music does much to set the mood of the western ranches. Through listening, children can enjoy and appreciate such relationships.

Reading music requires a readiness just as reading words does; before children are ready for this, they should have had a great number of musical experiences. They should have had the opportunity to listen to music, to make up their own music, and to sing other people's music; then they should be ready to recognize different notes. After these experiences, they will be ready to read the music of others. When children are forced into this before they are ready, poor attitudes, accompanied by a dislike for the music, will result. This negative feeling for music may persist throughout life.

Children love rhythm and movement. They love to sing little tunes that they have heard or have made up. They also love to move to music. Very often you will see a very young child in a crib or playpen swaying to music. And even at that very early age, they can clap their hands to music and find much enjoyment doing it. Children should not only be allowed but encouraged to do this, because not only is rhythm important to music, it is also important in reading, writing, and even talking. It is important that an aide or teacher does not put too many restrictions on a child's rhythm experiences. If the experience is too structured, it takes away from the enjoyment the child receives.

If you are assigned to work with children in rhythm activities but are not told exactly what to do, it would not be a problem for you since most things that move, move in rhythm, and you can ask the children to imitate these things. For instance, some things you can ask them to do are:

1. To be a bouncing ball
2. To be a circus horse
3. To be an ant
4. To be a rabbit
5. To be a turtle
6. To be a slithering snake
7. To reach as high as they can toward the sky
8. To make themselves as little as they can
9. To be a tree. To move their limbs—moving only their leaves
10. To be a cat slinking across the room, crouching to catch a mouse
11. To be a swimmer

As children get older, they will enjoy moving in more developed rhythmical patterns. Some of the things you can do for them at this age is to choose pieces of music which have clearly defined moods and let them interpret the moods through dance movements. Some suitable selections are *Peter and the Wolf, Grand Canyon Suite, Westside Story,* or almost any of the musical scores from children's musicals. Sometimes it is fun to tell the children part of a story and ask them to interpret it in dance. It can be a happy, sad, angry, or exciting story. They may invent dances to portray a holiday using scary movements for Halloween, a patriotic march rhythm for Independence Day, a slow, dignified, joyous dance for Thanksgiving, and lively springtime movements for Easter. The children can also interpret the movements of different occupations, such as a farmer, a miner, a train engineer, a typist, etc. Don't be discouraged if when you first introduce the idea, only one or two children are willing to take part. It won't be long until all the children will be begging for their turn to participate.

If children have had the opportunity to develop rhythmical movements, they will quickly particpate in more structured dances such as tribal dances, folk dances, and popular dances. The Virginia reel is a great dance to use as an introduction to folk dancing for older children. From there, the children will be excited and will be ready to go on to learn square dances, the schottische, and other dances.

The aide leads children in supervised rhythm activities, such as folk dances.

No matter what your talents and experiences are, there are many things you can do as an aide to help in the music program. Of course, if this is an area in which you are very competent, your participation and responsibilities will be increased. Setting up the music center may be your responsibility. Besides records, you may want to include some musical instruments, such as the Autoharp, melody and resonator bells, tambourines, finger cymbals, and triangles. Sometimes the music center includes homemade instruments for the children to play. These may be used to motivate the children to make their own instruments. You may have to keep this center supplied and change or add to the materials. Sometimes reference books, such as biographies of composers or source books on instruments are included here. The selection of books should be changed from time to time, too, as well as the records and instruments.

An aide who plays a musical instrument may be asked to help children during music lessons.

If you play an instrument yourself, especially the piano, you will be in great demand. But if you cannot play the piano, you can still be effective in the music program by using records, tapes, or asking the children to play instruments, if they can. Also you will find learning to play the Autoharp an enjoyable experience. The use of the Autoharp is very effective with children, especially in small groups. When you have learned to play the Autoharp, it will be fun

to teach some of the children how to use it. Perhaps at times you
will feel uncomfortable in some music situations if you feel you lack
musical talent. Remember, that the children do not expect a professional musician. They would rather have you with them and know
you are enjoying the experience. In that way, their enjoyment is
greater.

Art

If planning the school day were left up to the children, the day
might contain one art experience after another! If so, it could be a
very valuable day, for art does several very important things for children. The satisfaction of creating something is important to all of us,
and art gives children that satisfaction—if the classroom environment
is such that the children can explore and use various mediums. Art
allows the child a release from tensions and emotionally charged situations. While the child creates designs in finger painting or
pounds clay, or concentrates on the construction of a papier-mâché
object, the problems disappear for the moment and a sense of challenge, satisfaction, and serenity take their place. As children see a
painting of a lost child, they feel empathy and may be moved to
write a story about their feeling. As they construct a model of a mis-
sion church in a diorama, they do it with reverence, because they
begin to understand the feeling the missionaries had for it. As they
paint a card for their mother for Mother's Day, they experience the
desire to please someone. Art work is an opportunity for children to
express their feelings, and this important expression should be encouraged.

The aim in art is to help children realize their individuality and
uniqueness. They should be encouraged to create an object all their
own, rather than to try and produce a photographic copy of something. Patterns of objects which are to be traced have no place in a
creative art program. They stilt children's imagination, work, and
their ability to express themselves. Coloring books and mimeo-
graphed sheets for coloring are not art experiences. Adults who are
helping children in art must be careful about imposing their thoughts
on children. The children may be given the art problem, but it is
their job to solve that problem, and they must be allowed to do it in
their own way.

Children express themselves differently in art as they grow and
develop. Very young children express themselves symbolically in
many ways. They paint what they see, and they see things dif-

ferently from children who are a few years older and certainly differently from adults. For instance, the principal of a school once visited the kindergarten class, and the children painted pictures and wrote stories about the visit. In their pictures, they pictured the principal as a very tall person, reaching from the top to the bottom of the paper. The principal was really not very tall, but because of their point of view—as small children and as students in the presence of this authority—the principal was very tall. Sometimes, when little children paint pictures, they omit those things which do not appear important to them. For instance, if a visitor comes to the room and *talks* with the children, their drawings may be of a figure with a mouth but no eyes, no arms, and probably no legs. If their subject is doing something very important with his or her hands, the children may picture their subject with arms coming right out of the neck, with many, many fingers attached to the long arms. Trueness to size and perspective is not meaningful to young children. They see things in terms of tall or small, tiny or big, fat or skinny, long or short. The teaching staff should accept the children's giants or dwarves and continue to encourage them to paint exactly what they feel and see. As they grow and increase their powers of observation and communication, they develop more acuteness.

Although children should be left on their own to explore and create, there is a time to help them with techniques or skills. When a child is attempting to say something through painting but the brush won't say what the child wants it to express, the teacher or aide may move in to help. Perhaps the help is only sharpening the child's observation, or demonstrating a technique to use but it gets the child started and guides the child to a successful experience.

Children in the middle grades become more conscious of their art products, and more sensitive to the way in which others view them. Teachers and aides can help by suggesting ideas to them, urging them to develop a sense of composition and a sense of balance, or asking questions which will encourage the children to provide a focus in their paintings.

In the primary grades, art is used constantly to help the child communicate with others. In the upper elementary grades, art is often used for solving problems created by classroom work: storybook covers, scenery for plays and puppet shows, murals, posters, program covers, dioramas, and illustrations for reports.

Just as children should be given the opportunity to listen to beautiful music, so they should be given the opportunity to see art objects and fine paintings. Thus, the children would then have a

As children grow older, they become more self-conscious of
their art. This aide is helping children develop a sense of
composition in their work.

chance to discuss them and learn something about the artist. Not
only should paintings by the masters be included in the classroom,
but the paintings by the children should also be shown and perhaps
put on the bulletin board. The other children may borrow ideas
from these, but they will learn to incorporate only those techniques
they have seen in their own art work.

Of course, the types of materials and experiences children work
with in art should be in keeping with their ability and maturity. The
stages of growth in art expression are a very important part of the
developmental process.

The very first stage of self-expression is that of scribbling. This
begins long before the child has any wish to express an idea or
thought. The scribblings may vary from careless abandonment to
completely controlled movement. Some scribbles may be orderly
up and down strokes, some may be circular, and some may be just tiny
marks on the corner of the paper. At the end of this stage, when
they want some useful means of expression, children will seek out an
adult to share their drawings. They might begin to tell the adult
about their swing, their house, or their puppy. At this time, it is the
role of the teacher or the aide to provide the child with the materials
and encouragement needed. This is not the time to try to make the
child put more form in his or her drawings. The child does not yet
have the motor control or the coordination for this. Many times at

this stage adults tell children to stay within the lines. Unfortunately, children may come to feel that this is the main objective in an art experience.

Kindergarten children, in keeping with psychological development, are timid about trying new things and will very often sit back and say they can't when any experience is first suggested. When children do get involved, their scribbles become better controlled. Given many art opportunities, their scribbles turn into simple figures, and sometimes *baseline* even appears in the drawings. At this stage, the children's paintings tend to be limited and to focus primarily on themselves. They will show themselves in many different activities. The shape that children at this stage work with most often is the shape of the circle. A circle for a head, a circle for the body, etc. Soon a rectangle appears and then triangles. This is a stage of experimenting. The children are expressing themselves but aren't necessarily providing their audience with a masterpiece. Because of this, it isn't necessary to save and post all their pictures. In most cases, the value of these kinds of experiences is in the doing.

In the upper primary grades, children's drawings reach out to include other people. The children at this point begin to see themselves in relationship to the world. At this time, their academic skills are becoming more functional, and they are beginning to enjoy groups of children. At this time, too, the children may make x-ray pictures, that is, draw the inside and outside of the thing in the same drawing. They may also include many experiences in one picture, or more than one view of something. At this point, the children enjoy working "big" and will very often get down on the floor to do their paintings. They will also use a larger variety of art materials.

As children go into the intermediate grades, they have a whole new set of characteristics. The students begin to draw by using lines which are no longer geometric, but are not yet considered completely visual concepts. They begin to focus upon the characteristics of the different sexes. The girls may create glamorous girls in beautiful flowing gowns. Boys often draw large muscular football stars. The costume of the figure becomes very important. At this time, the child picks up certain sterotypes from advertising, TV, comic strips, or cartoons. To counteract this, the teacher may ask the student to draw figures of characters doing certain tasks or expressing certain feelings. At this stage, the child discovers the meaning of artistic concepts such as the plane and the baseline, and will no longer leave a space between the sky and the ground. This is natural, and the teacher and aide must have patience to wait until it happens. At this time, the children enjoy new art experiences such as crafts, puppetry, and ceramics.

Very young children usually paint very large simple shapes.
The subject matter is of things familiar to them.

Because some elementary school children will develop quickly
and will move into the preadolescent stage in art expression, it is
necessary to discuss this stage here. This is the phase where children sharpen their ability to observe visually. In some children this
is shown by a sketchy quality in their drawings; others include joints
such as knees, wrists, and elbows. Others become concerned with
correct proportions of the figure or object. Many learn to use light
and shadow or to show diminishing size. Some children's art will
show a combination of all these factors. The preadolescent child is
probably at the most critical point in creative development. At this
stage, the child is looking at his or her work with adult expectations,
but with the coordination of a child. Wanting to do something, but
without the ability to do it, may bring the creative work to a halt.
This is a difficult problem for the teacher and the aide to solve. The

best way to handle it is to point out positive qualities in the work and perhaps to ask questions about some good aspects in the art work: How did you manage to get the feeling of balance? How did you make the trees look so far away? In this way, the teacher or aide is giving approval and showing respect for individual differences. This strengthens children's confidence in their own creative endeavors.

Children may learn a variety of crafts which use threads. For example, these children are learning how to weave.

The only limit to the types of activities and art materials children work with is the child's maturity. Children of elementary school age must work with materials and tools which they can effectively control. To be more helpful in the classroom, the aide should become acquainted with these materials and learn how they are used. Some of the art experiences suitable for elementary school children are:

1. Drawing: pencils, crayons, charcoal, ink, and pastels
2. Painting: fingerpaint, tempera, powder paint, and water colors
3. Paper work: cutting, pasting, collages, papier-mâché, paper folding, and paper sculpture

4. Modeling: clay, salt dough, flour and starch dough, and papier-mâché
5. Construction: wood, plastic, and paper
6. Printing: wood, potato, linoleum, silk screen, and various fabrics
7. Thread crafts: weaving, macrame, sewing, knitting, crocheting, and embroidering

Some of the supplies and equipment which are needed in the classroom for art activities include the following:[1]

1. Finger-paint base and dry-powder colors. Small jars with covers that have holes punched in them make good shakers for the paints if they are to be used dry.
2. Glazed paper—white wrapping paper glazed on one side—or white oilcloth for finger painting.
3. Old newspapers on which to put finished paintings to dry.
4. Tempera paints, either liquid or powder.
5. Stiff bristle brushes of good quality, flat furrule, ½, ¾, or 1 inch wide, with handles long enough to permit long sweeping strokes.
6. Large paper—plain or colored newsprint, wrapping paper, mill screening. Paper should be at least 18 × 14 inches, as smaller sheets hamper a young child's freedom in drawing.
7. Containers for mixed paints—glass jars, tin cans, milk cartons. Half-pint waxed paper milk cartons are preferable because they can be discarded when the paint is used—a new supply is always available.
8. Easels—stationary or portable. If easels are not available, pieces of chipboard or corrugated paper, propped up on the legs of an inverted chair, on the floor, on the chalk rail or on a window ledge may be substituted. Sheets of drawing paper may be taped to the chalkboard; however, a slanted surface is generally easier to work on than one that is vertical.
9. Sponges, cloths, paper towels for cleaning up. Newspapers may be spread on the floor to catch paint drips.
10. Aprons to protect the children's clothing. Plastic, oilcloth, cloth, or newspaper aprons may be used. Old shirts with the sleeves cut off, worn backwards, make useful aprons.
11. Fixatives—shellac and other protective materials are needed.
12. Chalk—white and colored. Materials must be nonpoisonous.
13. Wax crayons, large size, from 8 to 16 colors.

[1] Strickland, Ruth. *Teacher's Guide to Education in Early Childhood.* Sacramento: Bureau of Elementary Education, California State Department of Education, 1956, p. 413.

14. Water colors.
15. Enamel paints, turpentine, and linseed oil for use in decorating or painting things children make.
16. Paint brushes.
17. Electric iron (for smoothing finger paintings when dry).
18. Space for displaying finished productions.
19. Cupboards and files for storing finished paintings.

An aide gives children directions for a cut and paste activity.

Many art experiences such as collages, mosaics, and rubbings require scrap materials, and most teachers keep a box of scraps just for these. The materials which may be included are:

SCRAP MATERIALS

Metal foils	Boxes
Beads	Cans
Buttons	Cellophane

Burlap   Cloth remnants

Costume jewelry   Screening

Felt scraps   Spools

Feathers   String

Paper bags   Wallpaper books

Paper plates   Wire

Newspapers   Wood scraps

Ribbon   Yarn

NATURE MATERIALS
Pine cones   Shells

Burs   Reeds

Seeds   Bushes

Twigs   Pods

The following is a suggested list of some common art experiences, including the use of a variety of materials:

PRIMARY GRADES
Illustrate original stories or stories and poems you have read.

Make holiday decorations and greeting cards.

Make clay objects.

Do sculpture (from soap, pipe cleaners, rocks, etc.).

Make puppets (stick, finger, paper bag).

Prepare puppet shows, costume, and scenery.

Make murals and dioramas for social science and literature projects.

Make montages (from junk or other materials).

Make designs from cloth.

Draw portraits.

Do sawdust or papier-mâché modeling.

Paint scenery for plays.

Build models (forts, houses, missions, trains, farms).

Make gifts.

Make torn-paper and cut-paper designs.

Make masks (from paper plates, paper bags, papier-mâché).

Make stick prints.

Paint or color abstract ideas such as happiness, joy.

Make potato prints and block prints.

Sew yarn on burlap.

Make mobiles.

Make posters.

Do spatter painting, finger painting, or sponge painting.

Construct something (use curled paper, large cardboard boxes, wood, etc.).

Design maps.

Do crayon etchings.

Make chalk drawings.

Children can learn to make their own puppets. These children have written and are presenting a play using their handmade puppets.

Besides the list for primary grades, children in the intermediate grades are also likely to enjoy the following activities:

INTERMEDIATE GRADES
Make tiles.

Build forms over crushed paper.

Do felt pen drawings.

Do mosaics (from crushed glass, seeds, sand, etc.).

Make cartoon strips.

Make artificial flowers.

Satisfactory art experiences require thorough organization by the teacher. The locations used for art work, the art materials, and the children all need to be prepared. For some projects, the children need shirts to protect their clothing, and newspaper or plastic sheets to protect tables and floors. Some materials may have to be cut, paints need to be mixed, scissors or brushes need to be counted and grouped, glue and paste should be made available, an area for drying the art work may need to be assigned. Naturally, when the art activity is finished, all these things need to be collected, cleaned, and put away. No wonder many teachers cringe at the thought of art activities. However, with the help of a competent aide, everybody can enjoy the experience. Before an art activity begins, the aide and teacher should plan what the activity will be, what supplies are necessary, what equipment is necessary, and any other things which will have to be prepared. The first few times the aide performs this assignment, he or she should meet with the teacher before beginning preparations, and again when things are ready. If the aide has not understood the teacher correctly or has forgotten to do something, the teacher may realize and make the corrections. The teacher will probably include children in the preparation and cleanup activities. It will help the aide to know what responsibilities the children will have so that help can be given in carrying them out satisfactorily.

The aide can help in ways other than preparing for art projects. A box of scraps is a necessary supply item, and yet it is often ignored either because it is an unorganized kind of material or because of the poor selection of scraps available. The aide can take the responsibility for this box and can keep it in such condition that the children may find many useful items.

In many districts, there are some fine films and filmstrips available on various art techniques and experiences. If the aide is assisting in the art program, this source should not be overlooked.

There are many art appreciation activities and situations which help to stimulate creative thinking in children. The aide may be called upon to accompany a group of children on a *looking walk* to find beauty in line, form, color, texture, and pattern. As an aide, you may make flower arrangements in the classroom for a *beauty center*. You might collect materials for a *touching table* where children can enjoy the feel of articles: velvet, ribbon, soft toys, sandpaper, glass, worn stones, marbles, etc. You could arrange the bulletin boards displaying the children's paintings, or you can help children mount paintings. The library corner in the classroom should be a pleasant and attractive place to enjoy reading or just thinking. As the aide, you can arrange and decorate this corner. And, of course, the aide will be needed when the class takes a field trip to the museum or to art exhibits. The aide's main responsibility is to be a partner to the teacher in helping to bring out the child's original ideas and in helping to give the child confidence to express these ideas.

Chapter Summary

Creativity exists to some degree in everybody. However, in a society which tends to look for similarities, motivates to convergent thinking, and rewards conforming behavior, creative thinking is often lost. However, emphasis has recently been placed on creative growth. Although creativity cannot be taught, it can be encouraged. Creativity should not be limited to the arts. It should be developed in all areas of education. The setting for creative work should include a friendly atmosphere in the classroom, an absence of vigorous interpersonal competition, acceptance by the teacher or the aide of widely differing performances, and an opportunity for creative expression throughout the school week rather than only during one or two periods each week. Although creativity is to be encouraged in all other areas of the curriculum, a special effort should be made during the specific time scheduled for other subjects to develop the skills necessary in that subject. Creativity should be encouraged, but not at the expense of subject skills.

Music provides children with a creative means of communication. These means include singing and playing, writing songs and music, listening to and reading music, and rhythmical activities.

Art does several important things for children. Art supplies the satisfaction of creating something, and a release from tensions and emotionally charged situations. Art work is an opportunity for children to express their feelings, and it is important that art experiences be encouraged.

Art also develops children's cultural appreciation, creative expression, and perceptual, manipulative, and organizational skills.

Art helps children discover their individuality and uniqueness. Patterns for tracing have no place in a creative art program. Children should be encouraged to create an object all their own. There is a time and place when children need to be helped with skills and techniques. This comes when the children attempt to say something through painting, but the brush will not say what the they want to say. The skillful aide, through asking questions about the painting, or by expressing an interest in the work, can motivate the children to a satisfactory art experience.

The chapter includes lists of common art experience for the primary and intermediate grades.

Suggested References

Kelley, Marjorie, and Roukes, Nicholas. *Matting and Displaying the Work of Children.* Palo Alto, California: Fearon Publishers, Inc., 1968.

Koskey, Thomas A. *Creative Corrugated Cardboard.* Palo Alto, California: Fearon Publishers, Inc., 1957.

Liechti, Alice, and Chappell, Jack. *Making and Using Charts.* Palo Alto, California: Fearon Publishers, Inc., 1968.

Lowenfeld, Viktor. *Creative and Mental Growth.* 3d ed. New York: The Macmillan Company, 1957.

Romber, Jenean, and Rutz, Miriam Easton. *Art Today and Every Day.* West Nyack, N.Y.: Parker Publishing Co., Inc., 1972.

Senti, Marvel A. "Fundamentals in Art," *Fundamentals for Children in Our Time.* Lawrence: University of Kansas, 1954.

Shuster, Albert H., and Ploghoft, Milton E. *The Emerging Elementary Curriculum Methods and Procedures.* Columbus, Ohio: Charles E. Merrill Books, Inc., 1963.

Smith, James A. *Creative Teaching of the Creative Arts in the Elementary School.* Boston: Allyn and Bacon, Inc., 1967.

Introduction

The idea of using teacher aides in the classroom probably began with the use of paraprofessionals as yard supervisors. This was one of the first demands of professional teachers. They insisted that it does not take a college degree to supervise children on a playground. They wanted some relief provided in this area so that they could use their professional know-how more capably in the classroom.

Districts were slow to accept this demand. Their first step was to approve of paraprofessionals as yard supervisors on the playground, but they insisted that a credentialed person must also be there. This proved to be a wise decision because it became apparent almost immediately that some skill is involved in being able to supervise a playground effectively. Most teachers developed these skills along with their training and classroom experience. Their

playground supervision:
equipment and activities

6

competency in yard supervision was an almost automatic response to the situation. However, the yard supervisors, who were not teachers and did not have a teaching background, had some bad experiences. As a result, some aides never returned to the playground again. Teachers and administrators saw from this that some training was necessary. They were willing to give essential on-the-job training because they had already had the taste of how sweet it is to have duty-free lunch and recess periods. From this point, aides moved from the playground into the classrooms. Relieving teachers of nonprofessional duties outside made it possible for the next step, which was to relieve teachers of nonprofessional duties inside.

Although yard supervision may have been the first area in which aides were used, you must not assume that a yard supervisor needs no training. You may have supervised your own children and all their friends in your backyard. You may have even taken a cub-scout group on a hike. However, it is not quite the same as being responsible for a hundred or more children of differing ages in a variety of games, each one showing individual skills and needs, and each one having a definite idea of what the purpose of the recess period is. Do not panic. It is not an impossible situation. In fact, after you have had some basic pointers from a trained teacher, you may find it to be a very pleasurable one. This experience gives you the opportunity of getting to know children in a very different situation from that of being in the classroom. Children may open up and tell you things on the playground that they would never share with you in the classroom setting. In a team teaching situation, aides can often bring to a planning meeting some pertinent information about a child that they have discovered while on playground duty. Perhaps it was something the child told the aide; perhaps it was an alert aide's observation of a child in a less formal situation than the one the teacher experiences in the classroom. Be armed with background knowledge of what to expect from children, some knowledge about the rules of games, the rules of the school, and also enjoy your recesses as much as the children.

One mother who volunteered to help on the playground because she so enjoyed playing with her own young children checked in her whistle after two days on the intermediate playground with the comment, I didn't realize the older children were so different. They wander in gangs, their rules are too complicated, and they don't show respect. Perhaps, if she had had a better idea of what to expect from each age level, she would have been prepared for this and would have been better able to cope with the problems. She may even have enjoyed observing the developmental characteristics of children at the various age levels.

Facilities, Equipment, and Supplies

Facilities and equipment vary according to building sites, school budget, and district philosophy. However, you will work with some types of equipment and supplies at almost every school, so it will be well for you to know how they should be used.

Most schools now have separated playgrounds for the primary children and the intermediate children, and also a private playground for the kindergarten children. The playgrounds will be discussed here individually.

The kindergarten playground is usually attached to the kindergarten room so the children may move back and forth freely, thus making the playground an extension of the classroom. The kindergarten play area will usually have a surfaced area for using wheeled toys. This area can also be used for playing with blocks and painting. Kindergartners love a digging area, and they usually have one in addition to a sandbox. Some kindergartens have an area set aside for live pets. The equipment you will probably find on most kindergarten playgrounds will be some kind of climbing apparatus, swings with canvas seats, a slide with ladder, a balance beam, and a low horizontal bar. Children of kindergarten age use sandbox tools, large wooden blocks, sawhorses, small tables and chairs, wheel toys such as tricycles and wheelbarrows, workbenches, tools and scrap wood, single jump ropes, and rubber balls of various sizes.

The playground for the primary grades will have many of the same types of play areas the kindergarten one has. However, in addition, the primary playground will have surfaced court areas for dodge ball, relay racing and hopscotch, and squares and circles drawn on the court areas to serve for small group games. The primary playground has larger climbing apparatus, horizontal bars, and swings than the kindergarten playground. Monkey rings may be added to their playground. The primary children will also enjoy a sandy area to dig in, a kickball field, a tetherball court, and a grassy area. Their playground supplies include balls of various sizes, jump ropes, hula hoops, and bean bags.

The intermediate playground has horizontal bars, climbing apparatus, and monkey bars, but all built on a larger scale. The surface area on the intermediate playground will have tetherball and handball courts, room for circle games, and basketball and volleyball courts. There will also be softball or kickball diamonds, relay areas, space for jumping events, and a grassy area used for various activities. Supplies include balls of various sizes, ring and toss games, hula hoops, tumbling mats, and table tennis paddles and balls.

Children play on the climbing apparatus of the school playground.

It is most important that the aide know the school's rules in the use of equipment and supplies, and that those rules are observed at all times. First of all, train yourself to be alert to any dangerous situation which may occur, whether in the condition of the equipment of the ground or in the actions of a child.

It is the duty of any adult on the playground to help the children develop a sense of responsibility for the safety of others during activity periods.   Here are some safety suggestions to help guide you in your supervision.

1. Check the apparatus for rigidity, for loose nuts or bolts, or for broken parts.   If you find a problem, keep children off the equipment and report the problem to the office immediately.
2. Depending on the size of the apparatus, control the number of children that may use it simultaneously.
3. See that children use both hands when grasping bars on the climbing apparatus.
4. Check the pits beneath the horizontal bars and slides frequently to be sure no sharp object has fallen into them.
5. Help a child who is trying a new or difficult stunt on an apparatus.
6. Discourage swinging of traveling rings over the crossbars.
7. Insist that children wait their turn without pushing or going ahead of others in line.
8. Teach children how to use slides correctly: they should sit erect on the surface with feet together.   Make sure they slide this way.
9. Have children use steps to reach the top of the slide.   See that no one else is on the slide before they descend.   Be sure they leave the foot of the slide by walking forward out of the pit.
10. Do not let children kneel or stand on swing seats.   Allow only one child to use a swing at a time.   Do not permit empty swings to be pushed or twisted.   Do not let children bail out of swings.   Keep other children out of the path of swings.
11. Keep kicking and throwing activities in one area.
12. Do not allow other children to run through court areas.
13. Do not allow children to recover equipment from a busy or dangerous area.
14. Do not use sticks or stones for bases in games or to mark running areas.
15. Do not let children run to walls or fences as goals.

As the playground supervisor, you should observe the following rules:

1. Do not overuse the whistle.   When you really want the children's attention, you will not get it.   If you do blow the whistle, do it for a good reason, and demand that you get the necessary attention from the children.
2. When you are supervising in the playground, circulate around the playground.   Do not stand in one place and talk with another person.

Wander around the playground, visit hidden areas, and do not forget to supervise the rest room areas.

3. If a fight starts or an injury occurs on the playground, do not run to the location. Nothing stimulates children faster than to see an adult running. They will join you in your run, and then you not only have the original problem to deal with, but you have added complications. So walk, do not run!

4. Do not show favoritism when you are on duty. Do not always give equipment to the same child, or walk with the same child, or let one child disobey the rules when others are scolded for the same thing.

The aide is breaking up a fight in the school playground.

Playground Activities

games   Whether you are supervising the play area or working as an aide in a physical education class, the techniques of game leadership and the knowledge of a variety of games are essential to you.

Be an energetic and enthusiastic game leader. Students will reflect your attitude. Enthusiasm is contagious. Lead the games in a way which suggests you believe they will be good fun for the participants.

Confidence is another essential of successful game leadership. This grows out of experience and a thorough knowledge of the games to be played. Mastery of the rules of the game is your first step in developing confidence, assurance, and poise.

Individual differences are as important in the physical education program as they are in any other area of school life. With the help of aides, the physical education instructor can gear the physical activity program to the child's needs. To do this, the aide must be ready to assume game leadership.

The following suggestions are offered as techniques of effective leadership in games:

1. Be sure you have a plan for each game period and then follow your plan. The plan may be developed by the physical education instructor or by both of you.
2. Have all equipment ready and available.
3. Remember you are working with children, not games.
4. Stand in a position where you can be seen and heard by everyone. If some explanation is essential, speak clearly and simply, but emphasize only the difficult parts of the game.
5. Get the participants in proper position—circle, line, etc.—before you begin to describe or demonstrate the game.
6. In team games, clearly distinguish the sides by colored ribbons or armbands.
7. Get every game under way quickly. Do not explain if you can demonstrate. Do not demonstrate longer than is necessary to get the participants into the activity.
8. Make minor corrections of faults in play while the game is in progress.
9. Anticipate difficulties and demonstrate the solution, thereby reducing the number of questions and long delays in getting the game under way.
10. Stop the game before interest begins to lag.
11. Be alert to capitalize on unexpected happenings. Remember, however, laugh *with* the children, not *at* them.
12. Adjust teams so that they are equal in terms of height and weight for participation in strenuous activities.
13. In competitive events, use small groups to permit more activity. If you have a class of twenty, use four lines instead of two.

14. Establish definite starting, turning, and ending lines. Space lines far enough apart to avoid collisions and confusion.

exercises   Before children begin playing games, it is important that they have a brief warm-up or exercise period. The responsibility of leading the children through these exercises is very often left up to the aide so that the physical education instructor can use that time to make last-minute preparations. Here are some points to take into consideration when supervising the exercise program.

1. Do not introduce too many new exercises at once.
2. Do not do the exercises at too rapid a pace.
3. Do not increase too rapidly the number of times an exercise is given. Otherwise, you will tear down instead of building up the muscles.
4. Be sure of smooth transition from one exercise to another by hopping and skipping.
5. Be sure to use the exercise program regularly.

It is important that the exercise period include exercises which involve the arm and shoulder girdle, the abdomen, the back, the legs, the pelvic region, the general trunk muscles, and overall coordination of the gross muscles of the body.

If the physical education assignment is yours, study physical education books and begin a card file on some exercises suitable for children involving different parts of the body.

If your duties as a teacher aide include playground supervision or assisting with physical education classes, you will have a sense of security if you have a knowledge of various types of games which you can use at a moment's notice. Children love to learn new games, as long as they are not asked to learn too many too fast. One of the most important things you can do to improve your value as an aide is to begin a collection of games, relays, and exercises. Write them out on index cards and add to the collection when you have an opportunity. You will find physical education books and game books in the school professional library. Each month look through teachers' and children's magazines. You'll find many new games listed there.

Most intermediate children enjoy team sports such as softball, kickball, volleyball, soccer, and basketball. The official rules for playing these games are found in physical education handbooks, sports rules books, or encyclopedias. There are a few games some older children enjoy, especially as a break from more structured games. Children in intermediate grades are keenly interested in relays, and are physically and mentally ready for this highly competitive activity. Relays are varied. They can be played with or without equipment, in a stationary position, or when running. They are easily organized and supervised, but it is important for the leader to know the organization and rules of the different types of relays. Children are sensitive to rules and expect the leader to respond to them in like manner. The following suggestions are recommended for relay games:

1. Explain the relay so the children understand what they are to do.
2. Point out or mark the boundary lines so the children understand them.
3. Be sure the children understand which aisles they are to use after the exchange has taken place and the player returns to the end of the line.
4. If the teams do not have the same number of players, either equalize them or explain what other arrangements you have made.

It is important to know the official rules of team sports in order to supervise games.

Relays are planned to build certain skills. As you choose one, be sure you know what that skill is. Choose relays that develop those skills which are useful for the children you are supervising. Relay directions should be added to your card collection. On your card include at what age the child can participate in the relay games and what skill it is helping to develop.

The aide must be prepared with many indoor classroom games which children can play on rainy days.

Indoor classroom games can also include games which children can play in small groups.

Without a large repertoire of classroom games, the phrase *rainy day* can strike fear in the hearts of school personnel. What does one do with thirty children at recess time when they are not able to go out on the playground? The answer is simple—they play in the classroom. If the leader is prepared in advance with a wide variety of indoor games, the period can go smoothly. If not, and the children are left to their own entertainment for the recess period, the time can be chaotic. Be sure that your collection of games includes an ample supply of classroom activities.

You should prepare a list of classroom games which are suitable for various age groups. Use the same resources which you used for suggestions of team games and playground activities.

noon supervision   Since many states have adopted duty-free lunch periods for teachers, noon-supervision duty has been assigned to aides. This means supervising the lunchroom or school cafeteria during lunch periods. Before you begin this job, be sure to get an idea of what cafeteria procedures and standards the school has. It will help to know the answers to these questions:

1. Who is in charge of the cafeteria—the cook, the principal? If you need help, to whom do you go?
2. How are lunches sold, complete or à la carte?
3. What route do children use to get to the lunchroom, to the serving area, and to the tables?
4. Do some children bring lunches from home, and if so, what rules apply to them?
5. What are the rules concerning trading food, borrowing money, table hopping, leaving the cafeteria area, getting second helpings, returning service and trays, trays and food taken out of the lunchroom?

Lunchroom procedures vary in different schools. Sometimes children are assigned to certain tables. Some lunchrooms have hosts for each table. The hosts take care of any needs that may come up, such as extra silverware, second helping, etc. They are given the authority to excuse the children when the area has been cleaned. Some schools limit movement and talking, while other schools see this as a social gathering and encourage children to choose their table and take part in the table conversation. If you are in charge of the lunchroom, let your standards be guided by the kind of an environment you most enjoy while you are eating.

First Aid

In any situation where relatively large numbers of youngsters are assembled, emergencies will occur despite carefully planned and thoughtful precautions. The aide's principal responsibility lies in notifying the person in charge and then providing necessary care until that person arrives. If a child is hurt on the playground and you are not sure if she or he should be moved, *don't move the child*. Instead, send someone (and in most cases it will have to be a child, so pick a responsible one) to the office for help.

Playground supervision includes comforting children after minor accidents.

When you are first assigned to a school and are collecting needed information about the school, ask about the procedure to follow when a child is hurt. If the school has a nurse on duty at all times, you may be advised to talk with the nurse, who will be able to give you hints about safe playground supervision. If the school does not have a nurse, find out who has the nurse's responsibility. Usually it is the principal, but in some cases it is a trained teacher, custodian, or bus driver.

Remember, when a playground accident happens, keep cool. If you panic, so will a playground full of children. Do the things which need to be done, send for help, comfort the child, control the situation. Help comes quickly—it just seems like hours. If you are really concerned about this part of your job, you may want to take a first-aid course or become familiar with the first-aid handbook.

The playground aide's job is by no means an easy one. It requires a wealth of knowledge, an abundance of patience and understanding, and the desire and ability to motivate children to want to participate in activities that will build their bodies and character. It requires the ability to be good-natured and friendly without losing control, and the ability to discipline fairly. This is a large responsibility that cannot be taken lightly. However, for the aide who likes children and enjoys helping them grow through play and exercise, it will be a truly rewarding task.

Chapter Summary

The playground supervision area may have been where aides were first used. Teachers realized that the playground supervisor did not need to be a credentialed teacher and were more than willing to train nonprofessionals to supervise playground activities. This allowed teachers more time to do the things they were trained to do and thereby increase teaching effectiveness.

This use of aides led to the use of teacher aides in many other areas where they have since proved their capability. Although the area of playground supervision was probably the first in which aides were used, it by no means requires the least preparation and training.

The playground aide is usually supervising the activities of large numbers of children of varied ages, abilities, and interests, and should know the characteristics of boys and girls at each level.

The playground aide should also be familiar with games, exercises, and activities for both boys and girls at the different age levels, and should know their rules and regulations. A knowledge of facilities, playground equipment, and supplies, as well as the safety requirements and procedures for using and maintaining them, is of paramount importance.

The aide should know how to handle playground emergencies, such as fights or injuries. The action the aide takes—and in what manner it is done—will set the tone of the playground session and perhaps even of the classroom for that day. It is necessary for the aide to be prepared to help in case of injury. It is also necessary to know what *not* to do as well as what to do in these cases.

The playground aide's job is not easy. The aide must know, and often teach, team games and relays to children. The aide must motivate children to participate in playground activities. The requirements of a playground supervisor are friendliness, a good nature, and the ability to discipline fairly.

Suggested References

Arnold, Arnold. *Children's Games.* New York: World Publishing Company, 1972.

Edgren, Harry D., and Gruber, Joseph J. *Teacher's Handbook of Indoor and Outdoor Games.* Englewood Cliffs, N.J.: Prentice-Hall, Inc. 1963.

Edson, Tom. "Physical Conditioning Exercises for Primary-Elementary Grades." Unpublished booklet for Physical Education In-Service Workshops for Riverside County Teachers, Riverside County Superintendent of Schools Office, 4015 Lemon St., Riverside, California, August, 1969.

Farina, Albert M., Furth, Sol H., and Smith, Joseph M. *Growth through Play.* Englewood Cliffs, N.J.: Prentice-Hall, Inc., 1959.

First Aid Text Book. Garden City, New York: Doubleday and Company, 1953.

Gesell, Arnold, and Ilg, Frances L. *The Child from Five to Ten.* New York: Harper and Row, Publishers, Incorporated, 1946.

Hackett and Jenson. *A Guide to Movement Education.* Palo Alto, California: Peck Publications, 1967.

Mosston, Muska. *Teaching Physical Education.* Columbus, Ohio: Charles E. Merrill Books, Inc., 1966.

President's Council on Youth Fitness, Youth Physical Fitness. Part I and Part II, Washington D.C.: U.S. Government Printing Office, 1961.

Richardson, Hazel A. *Games for Elementary Grades.* Minneapolis, Minnesota: Burgess Publishing Company, 1958.

Van Hagen, Winifred, Dexter, Genevieve, and Williams, Jesse Feiring. *Physical Education in the Elementary School.* Sacramento: California State Department of Education, 1951.

Introduction

Instructional media are the tools of the trade for teachers. With recent advancements in educational technology the classroom has changed from a text-centered unit to a multimedia learning center. The trend is toward instructional materials centers staffed by media specialists.

Media centers include magazines, newspapers, pamphlets, charts, study prints, programmed instructional materials, realia (real things used in daily living), kits, art objects, art prints, globes, maps, transparencies, videotapes, slides, films, microfilms, and a whole array of devices. This chapter deals with some of the most common media and ways to use them.

In almost every school there is one person who is either in charge of or considered to be the most knowledgeable in the care of audiovisual materials. Ask your teacher who that person is and speak to him or her about your school's equipment and methods. Be sure you know the correct procedures for arranging to use equipment; the ways to care for and operate equipment; and where and when to retun it. Know what materials are available and where and how you can get them.

New audiovisual equipment is constantly being developed. Luckily, it all comes complete with an instruction book so that, together with basic knowledge of how the most common equipment works, you can learn to become a proficient audiovisual aide.

instructional media 7

In using any audiovisual equipment, follow the boy scout motto, Be prepared. Nothing will frustrate an aide or teacher more, or turn off students faster, than an unsuccessful audiovisual experience. The preparation steps are few and simple, but follow them strictly.

1. Know how to use the machine.
2. Have the materials ready before the children are called together.
3. If you are using students' help, be sure they know what their responsibilities are.
4. Prepare a comfortable room arrangement.

Recordings—Disc and Tape

One of the more effective ways of bringing the outside world into the classroom is through the use of recordings, either records or tapes. A large variety of materials are available for both types of recordings, and both types may be used with a listening station allowing the materials to be used in small groups or individually.

Let us first look at the record player and the records. Do not assume that because you can play records at home without any problems, you need not prepare yourself for record-playing activity at school. Schools have a variety of record players, some so simple that they play only one speed. Do not be caught with a record player that plays at one speed when you have a record that must be played at another speed. Other record players are very complex. Perhaps your assignment is simply to play a recording for the class, but when you get to the record player you are met with a large selection of dials, switches, and plugs. While you are trying to figure out what they all mean, the class has shifted completely out of control. Be sure you know the record player before you use it with a group of children.

Not only is it necessary to know the record player, but it is most helpful to have some idea of the materials which are available for record players. It is very difficult for teachers to keep up to date with all the new materials. You may be helpful by simply reviewing the materials which are in the school library or by reading over the catalog of materials available through the audiovisual center.

The opportunities for using disc recordings are many and varied. The kindergarten teacher may find the record valuable in stimulating children to move to music and express their interpretation of animal movements. The primary teacher may use story records, which are not only for the pleasure of having the children hear a story, but also to motivate a youngster in reading. The art teacher will use a record as a new stimulus in painting and drawing, asking the children to listen to the record and catch its mood. The English teacher may use records for presenting poems, plays, or stories or for playing part of a story for the class and letting them write the ending. The social sciences teacher can present a dramatized historical happening out of history for the class. The music teacher uses records for music appreciation or as background music for singers. The physical education teacher finds records necessary for teaching folk and social dancing. The math teacher may send one group to listen to a record on multiplication-tables drill while working with other children.

Although tape recordings are increasing in popularity, disc records continue to offer the following advantages: they are easy to play and cannot be erased accidentally; record players are available in most schools and many homes, and almost any child can operate the equipment; most records are made of break-resistant materials. However, disc records do require some care. Users must place the needle carefully on the record so that it will not be scratched and the record must be returned to its jacket for storage so that the surface remains dust-free.

The aide may be in charge of keeping a file of tapes and checking out tapes when children wish to use them.

Recently magnetic tapes have become popular in schools. Cassette recorders are becoming more popular, and schools are including them in resource centers. Tape recorders offer the same type of listening experiences as disc recorders. Their great advantage is that teachers and students are able to record materials themselves easily and with no extra recording equipment. Tape recordings also offer great fidelity of reproduction. They give the convenience of immediate playback without any additional processing. Mistakes are of no great consequence, as tape can be erased and used many times. The opportunities for classroom recording are many. A radio broadcast of importance to the class may be recorded and brought in for class discussion. This has some advantages over listening to the original. In a tape recording, the sound can be stopped at any point and can be either discussed then or played back later for clearer understanding. If the original broadcast is made during school hours, the tape can be made and used at a time convenient for the class.

Another important use of tape recording is in evaluating oneself. Both children and adults in the classroom may use it in this manner. When children listen to their own oral reading or reports, they can recognize their problems in articulating, phrasing, pausing, or mumbling. You, as an aide, can do the same. Record your storytelling or presentation to a group. As you listen to it, evaluate it on the basis of whether you would enjoy listening to it if you were a child. Another way you might use a tape recording is to help a child who has a particular reading problem. Record the child reading and ask your supervising teacher to listen to it with you and to give you suggestions for ways to help the child.

A class may take a tape recorder on a field trip and record interviews, sounds, or discussions to take back to the classroom for further study.

An exchange of tapes with schools in other states or countries provides the children with a view of another locale or culture.

Children enjoy listening to a taped story from their reading book. By listening to the tape and following along in their books, they see the words as they hear them spoken. In taping the story of "Jack and the Beanstalk," for example, you might introduce the story to the children on the tape by telling them that this is a story about a poor family—a young boy who lived with his mother. Let the children hold the storybook in their hands. Continue with the introduction a little further and then suggest that they listen to find out what Jack got in trade for the cow. Then let them listen to the taped reading of the story. If the children are very young, it would be wise to stop the tape from time to time to ask them some questions which have been answered on that part of the tape and then bring the children's attention to the picture on the next page and give some clues as to what will happen next. Continue this for the rest of the story. Ask the important questions at the end of the story. Do not forget to ask if the children liked the story and why. Worksheets may be developed to go with the tapes using the same questions that you used asked as the children listened to the tape.

Recording on a tape recorder is not difficult, but it is more successful if you follow these suggestions:

1. The best recording distances and positions for the speaker in relation to the microphone are usually 6 to 18 inches directly in front of the "mike." Test this by speaking and recording (experimentally) from various spots around the microphone. This should be done for each voice being recorded.

2. Speak in a clear, distinct conversational manner. Don't shout or strain your voice. Remember you want the recording to sound natural and conversational. Voice inflections are important if your recorded voice is to sound natural.

3. If possible, eliminate undesired background noise. The sensitive, nonselective microphone will pick up and record these sounds. Classroom whispers, squeaking chairs, sounds of rattling paper (especially scripts near the mike) and shuffling feet, and all other noises are likely to be included in the recording.

4. Because of the microphone's sensitivity, don't jar or move it during the recording. Jarring or even brushing the mike and cord may be enough to cause a loud noise on the recording. *Always* handle a microphone with care.

5. Make your recordings in a room without excessive echo quality.

6. Guard against interruptions. It might be helpful to hang a big sign on the door with a warning like "Recording Inside—Please Do Not Disturb."

7. Bear in mind that many of the smaller tape recorders are not equipped to do complex recording jobs. Some have no provisions for monitoring, or listening back, as materials are being recorded. This is necessary if you are trying to "mix" several sounds into a recording of good quality.[1]

---

[1] Dale, Edgar. *Audiovisual Methods in Teaching.* 3d ed. New York: The Dryden Press, 1969, p. 495.

Check the instructions on how to use the machine, ask for help, and then practice using the machine before you use it with a group.

The Listening Center

Listening centers may vary. A high school or college may develop a specially equipped room for foreign language teaching. This may have enough booths or seats for an average size class. The center may be called a language laboratory. It may have a console in the room that the teacher can use to play one or more tapes or recordings. Pupils may or may not be able to record what they are saying. Teachers are able to listen to each individual pupil's response and communicate with the student to correct and instruct him or her. It is likely that the language textbooks used will have accompanying tapes for use in the laboratory.

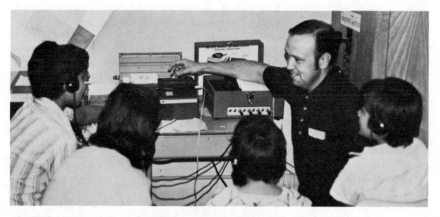

The aide may set up a listening center such as the one shown here. Children can use earphones to listen to records or tapes without disturbing the rest of the class.

Elementary schools usually have *listening corners,* sometimes called *listening centers* or *listening stations,* set up around the room. A record player or tape recorder may be equipped with distribution boxes containing several jacks into which earphones are plugged. This arrangement permits one or more students to listen to recordings without disturbing others. Through the use of listening posts, many learning activities can be taking place in a classroom without disturbing other students in the class. When a child is listening to a lesson over the earphones, all other noises in the classroom are inaudible. This is a one-to-one relationship. To make the listening center effective, rules for the use of the equipment must be made and obeyed.

The Overhead Projector

The overhead projector has become more and more popular in recent years due to the technological advances in machines and materials for making transparencies. The main advantage of an overhead projector is that the operator can project images on a large screen without having to darken the room. The door is open for imagination, innovation, and creativity in presentations. Commercially prepared transparencies in a large number of subject areas are readily available. Transparencies from most printed materials or hand-drawn materials may be easily and inexpensively prepared by the teacher or teacher aide. Sometimes as a learning experience, students prepare transparencies. Before preparing transparencies from printed materials, be sure that you are not violating copyright laws.

The operation of the machine is quite simple. However, it is very important that the machine be set up and used correctly. The machine should be placed at the front of the group with the image being projected either to the side or over the head of the operator. This allows the operator to either sit or stand and still face the audience. The size of the image will depend on the distance the projector is from the screen. If the bottom of the screen is closer to the projector lens than to the top, the image at the bottom will necessarily be smaller than the image at the top and will produce what is called a *keystone* effect. This can be eliminated by tying the bottom of the screen farther away from the projector. It is desirable to have the screen permanently mounted and the projector ready for instant use at all times. The operator must be careful not to get in the way of the image being projected because it will distract the children and cut down on the effectiveness of the presentation.

When the overhead projector is to be used as a substitute for the chalkboard, it should be equipped with a transparency roll. The operator can then write or draw on the transparency, using any number of colors or grease pencils to create the desired effect. A turn of the crank will clear the screen. This process is easier and quieter than erasing the chalkboard. Also if the transparency is needed later for reference, it is easily cranked back into position.

The operator can point out details on the screen by using a pencil on the transparency. The image of the pencil is then projected on the screen as a large pointer. A colored grease pencil or felt pen may be used to underline for emphasis.

In operating the projector, use the on-and-off switch to transfer attention to and from the operator and the screen. When the machine is turned on, the children's attention will immediately go to the screen. When it is turned off, their attention will go back to the operator.

When presenting a list of items or a number of ideas on one transparency, you may not want to present all the items at once. By placing a sheet of paper over the transparency, you may slide it down at your own pace to reveal only the items you want to show. This will help the children concentrate on one item at a time.

Another method of making a presentation without presenting everything at once is by using overlays. Use several transparencies that are hinged together in loose-leaf or book form to keep them in proper sequence and place. The first part you wish to present should be on the first transparency. Follow this by as many parts as you wish to add until the finished product is presented. This process allows for building a concept part by part. Whether sheet transparencies are used individually or in multiples, they should be mounted in cardboard mounting frames, marked well, and stored right side up in sequence so they are readily available.

Transparencies can be easily made by writing or drawing directly on clear acetate with various colored felt pens or grease pencils. Felt pens produce a better transparency than grease pencils because the width of lines and thickness of letters can be better controlled. Most felt pens have a water-base ink, and their markings can be removed with a moist cloth. Some felt pens have permanent ink and require a solvent for removal. Grease pencil markings can be removed with a dry cloth. The main drawback to handmade transparencies is the difficulty in obtaining good-quality drawings and lettering.

Heat-process transparencies are one of the most popular production methods used in schools today. They are produced from written, typed, drawn, or, if permission is available, from printed materials. These are transferred to transparency film by the use of copying machines that have an infrared light source. It takes only a few seconds for the original, placed in contact with a sheet of heat-sensitive film and run through the machine, to produce a transparency ready for the projector. Depending on the film used, the images may be black, any one of a number of colors, or in negative film. Not all printing or marking can be used, however; spirit duplicator copies, ordinary ball-point pens, and colored printing inks cannot be reproduced by this process. The originals must be prepared with heat-absorbing materials which include a soft-lead pencil, a good typewriter ribbon, black printing ink, and India ink.

This process may also be used to make a transparency from a duplicator master. Before making spirit duplicator copies, run the master through the machine together with a sheet of finely etched acetate. The machine will pick up the carbon markings from the master, just as paper does, resulting in a translucent transparency the color of the original duplicating master. This then can be used in conjunction with the paper copies given to the students.

When preparing transparencies, make sure that detail and printing are not too small for the children to see clearly. A primary typewriter with a good ribbon makes excellent printing that is easily read at a distance. Inexpensive materials and devices such as templates, stencils, ruling pens, brush pens, cutout letters, scribes, and many other items are available. By using these materials and devices, quality transparencies can easily be made. Do not use a regular typewriter to make transparencies, as even the largest standard type is too small to be seen by the audience.

It has always been thought that x-ray film belonged only in a doctor's office. Not so! Processed (exposed) x-ray film makes excellent do-it-yourself transparencies if you write or draw on it with one of the colored transparency marking pens. Other effective writing instruments are bowling-type scoring pencils, glass-marking pencils, and water-base markers.

If you want to make a quick permanent transparency, use a piece of ditto paper, a No. 2 lead pencil, and a good idea. If you hand-letter your transparency, remember to use large letters so they can be read at a distance. A maximum from ½ to 1 inch is usually sufficient. To make a good transparency, use one idea and keep it simple. It is more effective to make two transparencies with one good idea than one transparency with two ideas that must be unscrambled by the students.

A crossword puzzle or a map from a newspaper or some other printed source will make a good transparency. Make a ditto master as well as the transparency, and give the students a copy at the same time.

Remember that transparencies are like any other audiovisual materials. They require systematic planning and preparation. Before you set about making your actual transparencies, always consider the planning checklist:

1. What purpose will your transparencies serve?
2. What factors are important to consider about the children who will see the transparencies?
3. Are transparencies the best medium to accomplish your purposes and to convey the content?
4. Might transparencies be combined with other media for greater effectiveness?
5. Have you organized the content and made sketches to show what is to be included in each transparency?

The Filmstrip Projector

In certain cases, filmstrips can be as effective as motion pictures, especially when used in combination with other instructional materials. The advantage of the filmstrip is that the speed of the presentation can be adjusted. If the child should encounter difficulties in understanding an explanation or a sequence, the frame may remain projected on the screen until the child understands the explanation.

The aide helps a child select a filmstrip.

Filmstrips are used in many ways in classroom teaching and learning. They can be used in a whole class presentation, in small-group activities, or in individual student use. Very often filmstrips are put in a learning center, and when children begin using the center, they take the filmstrip to the viewing station and run it themselves. Filmstrips are a good way to initiate a concept, reinforce skills, or culminate a unit. Children should be reminded to use filmstrips when they are working on research projects. Children should also be reminded often of the care and correct use of filmstrips.

Learning centers are often equipped with filmstrip projectors. Here an aide is showing a child how to operate a projector.

Some filmstrips are becoming more popular in the classrooms. There are several kinds. The newer sound-filmstrip projector uses a filmstrip that has a sound track printed on it. This is easy to use and a very effective teaching device. If your school does not have this yet, you can substitute an ordinary film strip projector and either tapes or discs. These come as sets. On the recording a narrator explains and elaborates on the pictorial and graphic material. One of the problems with this method is starting the filmstrip and the recording together and keeping them that way throughout the showing.

The confusion which results when this is not done—when the picture is a frame or two ahead of or behind the sound—becomes one of the aide's most discouraging experiences. Some of the sound-filmstrip projectors have an electronic signal which causes the filmstrip frames to advance at a predetermined rate. This improves the realism of the sound-filmstrip presentation, eliminates the beep sound which is used to signal the operator to move the filmstrip to the next frame, and eliminates the problem of the film and the sound advancing independently of each other.

Filmstrip projectors are available in several different sizes, ranging from hand viewers to small-group projectors to projectors which will accommodate large crowds.

The Slide Projector

Slides are single, transparent pictures that are projected onto a screen for a small group or the entire class. They are usually taken on photographic film, although sometimes they consist of drawings on etched glass or plastic. Slides can often be shown with the same projector as is used for filmstrips, but with an accompanying attachment.

Slides have some of the same advantages or filmstrips. Each can be projected for an extended time, allowing the class to inspect details of the scene and to discuss it at length. They are easier to store than books, charts, or posters, and are relatively low in cost. Operating the projector is a simple matter.

Slides have these particular advantages: An instructor may make his or her own slides suited to the particular class needs. Also, if one or two scenes in a series of slides become out of date, they can easily be removed or replaced. If a teacher wishes to show only selected scenes from the sequence, he or she can do so readily.

Modern automatic slide projectors have trays that serve both as storage boxes for slides and as part of the slide-feed mechanism itself. These trays keep slides in proper sequence ready for projections. Some fully automatic projectors also change slides at predetermined rates; others include remote push-button slide change controls. All may be manually operated if desired.

Motion Picture Projector

The motion picture projector is used extensively in schools. Motion pictures have several important advantages in teaching, and should be used in ways which capitalize on them. They act upon two senses at one time which contributes to effective learning. Pupils may find it difficult to understand or experience concepts through discussion alone, but may learn from a well-organized, moving, and colorful film presentation.

An aide prepares to show a 16-mm film to the class. Motion picture projectors are used widely in schools.

Films provide a continuity of action. They can take the viewer anywhere in the world. Pupils can visit with all the peoples of the earth, mountains, deserts, forests, plants, and animals without having to leave the classroom. Special photographic techniques such as microphotography and animation extend the limits of normal human experiences. With the variety of films available, every curriculum area can be enriched.

8-mm Movie Projectors and Cartridge Projectors

The 8-mm movie projector is being used more and more in classrooms. The cost of both film and projector is considerably less than of the larger 16-mm projector. In addition, it is easier to use and store.

The 8-mm projectors are often used in what is generally referred to as *single-concept* films. These are cartridge films or film loops. They are continuous and allow the child or class to see the single concept over and over until it is mastered.

The super 8-mm projector uses the same film, but more of the film is exposed, giving a larger image and a clearer picture. Super 8-mm film cannot be used in the older 8-mm projectors, but newer projectors can use both.

Although most 8-mm and super 8-mm films are not equipped for sound, some of the newer films are equipped with either optional sound or magnetic sound tracks. The optional sound track is permanent and cannot be erased. The magnetic sound track may be erased at any time and new sound recorded on it.

The Opaque Projector

The opaque projector is unique since it requires no special preparation materials. Flat, printed, or drawn pictures, or other materials, as well as some three-dimensional objects may be projected on a screen instantly. Pages from books or magazines do not need to be removed to be projected. The opaque projector will project anything which can be framed in a maximum of a 10×10 inch area.

If a large group is viewing the projection, the room must be darkened. However, if only a small group is seated closely around the screen and the materials projected are of fairly large detail, the projection may be quite satisfactory in normal light.

Some of the typical applications of the opaque projectors are:

1. Project pictures or pages from a book or magazine.
2. Project students' papers for teacher or class comment.
3. Project drawings made by students, teachers, or aides.
4. Project to make large size drawings from small drawings. Examples would be: (a) a map of the United States projected on a chalkboard and copied with chalk or on butcher paper on the bulletin board, (b) a scene projected on canvas and copied to serve as a backdrop for a play, and (c) lettering projected onto a poster board to be copied to ensure high-quality lettering on signs.
5. Project small instruments such as slide rules, micrometers, and other scales. The group can watch the instrument being manipulated.
6. Project words of a song for sing-along activity.
7. Project a picture, letters, or other printed items onto a bulletin board and copy them by using different materials.

Chalkboards

At one time all chalkboards were made of black slate, so the use and care of boards were uniform. This is not true today. As you enter a classroom, you will notice chalkboards made of different materials and in many different colors. The characteristics of these boards vary. Not all chalks may be used on all boards, nor are all chalkboards cleaned the same way. Some require different cleaning methods and different erasers. Check with the school custodian before you try to clean the chalkboards.

The big advantages of the classroom chalkboard are that it is handy to use, it is always readily available, the information on the board will stay in view until you take it off, words and phrases can be emphasized by using different colored chalk, and it is not necessary to prepare it ahead of time.

Bulletin Boards

Since bulletin boards are often the responsibility of the aide, it may be valuable for you to look at materials available on bulletin board arrangement.

Bulletin boards should be springboards to new experiences, inquiry, investigation, and involvement. They can serve more than the eye by tempting children and arousing their curiosity. They can also offer challenges for independent study. Few children can resist touching, working, pushing, pulling, matching, or peeking into or under an attractive bulletin board display.

The aide has the job of keeping bulletin boards current, neat, and attractive.

Consider these ideas for perking up a board:

Try using different materials for backgrounds. It will be a welcome relief from the usual construction paper background. Tissue paper, for instance, is inexpensive and comes in many happy colors. Do not forget black paper. It provides a very effective contrast to any other color. If you are doing a special unit, use an unusual background, such as burlap or corrugated paper. The want-ad section of a newspaper provides a graphic background for current events bulletin boards.

Do not overlook a border. It serves to enclose the idea you are presenting, and offers another opportunity to make the board attractive. A quick border can be put up in a very short time. Use your stapler to edge the board with two strands of heavy, brightly colored yarn. Crepe paper twisted gently will also be attractive.

Children love three-dimensional boards. They are not hard to construct. Consider such things as attaching a peephole show to the board. A diorama made in a shoe box presenting a scene from a library book can motivate many to check out that book and read it. Use some realia—attach beehives, star fish, round leaves, or egg shells to a board. Science offers a whole array of ideas for bulletin boards. Use science equipment such as a magnifying glass with things to look at, magnets with objects to test, bead models of molecules to match with chemical formulas, or test tubes in which plant specimens can be placed. Attaching these things can be easy. Most of them can be hung from strands of yarn pinned to the board. Use paper sleeves to attach such things as test tubes to the board.

Flip-up displays are intriguing to children. On the outside of a circle, put a picture of a famous person. When the outside circle is flipped up, have a chart character sketch about the person. Many students will be interested only in the picture on the outside. Others will be more curious. The children who are especially interested in the subject will flip the top up and be grateful for the facts beneath.

Do not overlook the opportunity of getting the children into the bulletin-board act and into the behind-the-scenes learning that goes with it. Children can make strip-stories on rolls of shelf paper which can then be placed on a bulletin board. Children will be encouraged to research a topic for a strip-story. Children may also enjoy researching the size and distance of planets and then constructing a solar-system bulletin board in three dimensions. Sometimes a board can be reserved for children who request some way to present part of their knowledge to other children. Maybe it is a bulletin board about a student's hobby or a trip taken or whatever it is that interests that student at the moment. Perhaps the student wants to illustrate a social sciences report, put up math puzzles, draw characters from a favorite book, or introduce a new physical education activity. The important thing is that the bulletin board is of the student's own choosing.

Do no underestimate the importance of bulletin boards. They can help set the mood of the classroom. Be sure you understand the function of the bulletin board, the school's policies on bulletin boards, and the teacher's objective for their use. Remember that children, teachers, and visitors are affected by the bulletin boards. Keep them meaningful, attractive, and current.

Pegboards

The framed pegboard offers the classroom a teaching aid which may be used to make three-dimensional objects that may vary in size and weight almost without limitation. A pegboard consists of sheets of masonite (hard-surfaced pressed wood) which have holes drilled at 1-inch intervals across the surface. You cannot staple or pin material directly to the board. Rather, you use pegs that look like golf tees or a variety of wire fixtures that can be inserted in the holes to hold pictures and a great range of three-dimensional objects like books, jars, boxes, and specimens. Pictures can be taped to the hard surface. The pegboard provides for displays that can be put up and taken down or completely changed with ease and speed. It may be hung against a wall or bulletin board, or coordinated with a table exhibit.

Pegboards may be used in all classroom situations, from kindergarten through college, to display surfaces for art objects, sharing experiences, screens, or storage racks for single tools, rhythm instruments, or various other educational aids. With the wide variety of pegboard hooks available, it is possible to exhibit items of almost any size or shape.

Felt and Flannel Boards

The flannel board is a very effective teaching aid. The children enjoy seeing the figures stick to the board and are pleased with the very vivid colors available in felt. Flannel boards have many uses. A teacher can use it to present a lesson, a group of children may work with it, or it may be part of a learning center and used by individuals.

Most classrooms have at least one flannel board. In many rooms teachers use many of different sizes that they themselves have constructed. Boards can be made easily by attaching felt or flannel to any kind of board, plywood, cardboard, or masonite, or even by attaching flannel to a wall bulletin board.

Commercially prepared felt letters can be used effectively on flannel boards. Here an aide uses a flannel board to teach the alphabet to Spanish-speaking children.

If a teacher is not using a flannel board, it is not because it is not useful, but more likely because there is no time to construct the cutouts. This is another duty that an aide can take over.

Many commercially prepared materials are available for felt boards, such as felt letters, numbers, math symbols, animals, and other figures. A teacher might want many others but may not be able to buy them. They can be easily and inexpensively prepared. Most of the materials are at hand in every school and can be prepared quickly.

The materials need to be self-adhering materials such as felt, flannel, yarn, flocked paper, corduroy, suede, pipe cleaners, string, velvet, and many other types of yardage. When selecting materials, be sure to test to see if they can support their own weight on the board.

Very often a lesson will be written on paper which will not stick to the board. To take care of this, an adhesive flocking paper is available which can be attached to the paper so paper cutouts can be used. When fixing such an item, make sure there are enough flocking materials on the paper so that it will support the weight of the item.

When you are preparing cutouts for the board, you will want to color or write on them. This is possible. If you are using paper, you can use different colored paper, poster paint, felt markers, crayons, water paints, or ink. If you are going to mark on cloth, poster or casein paint can be used. Enamel paint can be used on rough surfaces. Colored chalk or pastels are very vivid and may be used very satisfactorily if the color is *fixed* with a commercial fixative. Otherwise the color will rub off. Before applying any kind of color to a cutout, test the materials first. Many times the cloth is too absorbent, so outlines may not be sharp enough.

You must prepare very carefully before you can present an effective flannel board lesson. The first step, of course, is to plan the lesson in accordance with the learning objective. Write out or chart out the steps of the lesson. If each child should have some materials such as information or questions, prepare these materials, and make duplicate copies for each student. The next step is to prepare the cutouts. After they are prepared, lay them out on a flat surface in their correct sequence and then number them so they will not be mixed up during the presentation. To help keep them in order and together, keep them in an envelope and label the envelope. The inexperienced aide or teacher should rehearse the presentation before class. During the rehearsal, the proper placement, timing, and continuity can be checked.

As was mentioned earlier, not only are felt boards used for presentation of lessons, but they are often available for student use. One example of this may be to draw an outline map on a large piece of felt. With this as the background, many different map skills and concepts can be learned. For instance, cutouts of various products turn it into a product-map activity; geographic symbols help a child get a better picture of the placement of mountains, lakes, plains, etc. In teaching the concept that environment influences the way Indians lived, cutouts can be made of the various Indian homes and placed in their correct location on the map. Music staffs can be drawn on felt and the cutouts can be different note symbols, and the children can try various activities placing the notes on the staff. Punctuation-mark cutouts are used to help children learn the use of punctuation in a sentence. Mathematical problems are more fun when they are worked on a felt board. The board can also be used for games, such as tic-tac-toe. You can see by these suggestions that many things are possible with the felt board. So experiment and enjoy using one.

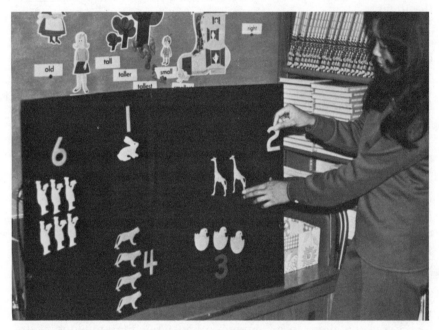

The aide is preparing a flannel board to help children understand numbers.

The Magnetic Board

A new teaching aid is the magnetic board. Instructors and students are able to create desired effects or build learning situations as the entire class observes. An assortment of magnets, some cardboard, scissors, a tube of cement, and a metal for displaying the magnetic symbols—the necessary equipment—need not present a problem, since many classrooms are already equipped with steel chalkboards. If the classroom does not have a metal chalkboard, improvise by framing a sheet of metal or a piece of screen wire. Magnetic accessories including chalkholders and erasers are available for preparing magnetic displays.

Magnetic boards can be used for recognition of numbers, colors, and objects, as well as word association when symbols on magnets are used. Music is a subject that is readily adapted to magnetic teaching methods. Magnets can serve as a practical teaching tool for visualizing geometric facts. Similarly, arithmetic and algebra are made more interesting with magnetized numbers and symbols. History, science, and other subjects may be illustrated effectively with magnetic symbols. There is no limit to using the magnetic board.

Learning Centers

Many kinds of instructional media are used in a learning center. In an open classroom environment, learning centers are set up for children to use with very little, if any, teacher supervision. A learning center is a space in the room (a table, desk, counter, bulletin board, etc.) equipped with instructions, activities, and materials for children to learn a specific skill. Centers are set up with a certain purpose or objective in mind.

Developing a center can be broken down into four parts:

1. Choosing the purpose of the center
2. Choosing the activities needed to meet that objective
3. Gathering and displaying the materials
4. Correcting, evaluating, and record keeping

A center can be used to introduce a new concept, to reinforce previous learning, or to expand interests. The center can be set up for certain individuals, groups of children, or everyone in the class with materials ranging in difficulty levels. The teacher will decide the purpose of the center and the children who will participate at the center. Both the teacher and the aide will gather the materials to equip the center.

Centers can include many different things. One of those is a bulletin board. The bulletin board may be used to display directions, explanations, samples, materials, or a combination of these. A bulletin board may be more than just the flat surface. Envelopes, pockets, and boxes attached to the board provide places to hold cards, display objects, and to hold supplies.

Children choose their own books in a reading learning center.

Centers contain *job cards*. These are cards that simply state the tasks the student is to perform. In addition, the materials needed to perform the activity are listed. Sometimes the answers to the tasks are put on the card so the student can have an immediate check.

Activity sheets or work sheets are also included at a center. Most often these will be of several different types, all aimed at the same objective by varying in difficulty and interests.

Centers also include learning games and such audiovisual materials as filmstrips, sound tapes of records, study prints, or slides. It is not necessary to have the audiovisual equipment to use these materials at every center. Instead, a station housing a projector, recorder, or game boards is set up, and the children take the tape,

An up-to-date picture file available to the students may be a
valuable part of a learning center.

film, etc., from the center to the station and return it when they are
finished.

Each center should have a folder for each child to put his or her
completed work, or there should be a folder station where a child
can deposit all his or her center's work.

Learning centers are another way of enabling the teacher to
work more effectively with individual differences within the class.
However, centers require constant modification and maintenance.
It is very difficult for teachers to find time to keep learning centers
current, and therefore this can be one of the most important contribu-
tions an aide makes to the classroom.

Chapter Summary

Instructional media are defined as *tools of the trade* for the teacher. They include books, magazines, papers, pamphlets, charts, study prints, programmed instructional materials, realia, kits, art objects, art prints, globes, maps transparencies, videotapes, slides, films, microfilms, and any number of machines and devices used for instruction.

New media are being created constantly. Old media are becoming obsolete as new technology is developed. Some large schools have a large quantity of instructional media usually kept in the media center and managed by a full-time media specialist. Smaller schools usually house the media in the classrooms, and the teachers share many items. In most situations, however, one person is considered more knowledgeable in this area than the rest. The aide should seek out this person to determine what media are available and where and how to get them. It is also important that the aide learn how to use and care for media. The aide must make sure that the media are returned on time and to the right place.

Items including recorders, record players, listening centers, overhead projectors, filmstrip projectors, slide projectors, opaque projectors, chalkboards, bulletin boards, pegboards, felt boards, flannel boards, magnetic boards, and learning centers have all been discussed in this chaper and are considered to be of lasting value. The aide should carefully study the information given on each of these items in the chapter and occasionally review the chapter to ensure that the media are being used advantageously.

Suggested References

Brown, James W., and Harcleroad, Fred F. *Audiovisual Instruction: Media and Methods.* New York: McGraw-Hill, Inc. 1969.

————*Audiovisual Instructional Materials Manual, A Self-Instructional Guide to Audiovisual Laboratory Experience.* New York: McGraw-Hill, Inc. 1969.

Dale, Edgar. *Audiovisual Methods in Teaching.* 3d ed. New York: The Dryden Press, 1969.

Forte, Imogene, Pangle, Mary Ann, and Tupa, Robert. *Center Stuff for Nooks, Crannies and Corners.* Nashville, Tennessee: Incentive Publications, 1973.

Gurske and Cote. *Learning Center Guide.* Sunnydale, California: CTM Co., 1972.

Koskey, Thomas A. *How to Make and Use Flannel Boards.* Palo Alto, California: Fearon Publishers, Inc., 1961.

Morlan, John. *Classroom Learning Centers.* Belmont, California: Lear Siegler, Inc. Fearon Publishers, 1974.

Waynant and Wilson. *Learning Centers—A Guide for Effective Use.* Paoli, Pennsylvania: The Instructo Corporation/McGraw Hill. 1974.

index

204

Relay games, 165
Relief maps (*see* Map making)
Report standards, 66
Reporting skills, 51–53
Reports, writing, 66–67
Rhythm activities, 139–140
Role playing, 54–55
Round-table discussions, 50

S

Salt-and-flour modeling material, 97
Sawdust mâché for map making, 97
Scheduling, flexible, 11
School system, 3–5
  organization of, chart, 3
Schools without Failure (Glasser), 88
Science, 104–114
  conceptual schemes, 106–113
Science materials, 113
Selective reading plan, 77–78
Self-evaluation:
  by children, tape recorders and, 176
  by teacher aides, form for, 39, 41–42
Singing (*see* Music)
Slide projectors, 184
Social sciences, 82–93, 114
Social Studies for Children in a Democracy (Michaelis), 99n.
Social Studies from Theory to Practice in Elementary Education (Douglas), 95n.
Sound-filmstrip projectors, 183–184
Speaking, 48–56
  discussion groups (*see* Discussion skills)

Speaking:
  reporting, 51–53
  role playing, 54–55
  storytelling, 53
Speech problems, 55–56
Spelling, 67–70
  individualized programs, 69
Spelling tests, giving, 69–70
Spiral plan, 88, 90, 93
Staffing, differentiated, 2, 5
Story formula, 72
Storytelling, 53
Strickland, Ruth, 148n.
Superintendent of schools, 4

T

Taba, Hilda, 88
Tape recordings (*see* Recordings, tape)
Taxonomy of Educational Objectives (Committee of College and University Examiners), 90n.
Teacher aides:
  application form, 13
  and children (*see* Children, working with)
  evaluation of, 39
    evaluation form, 41–42
    rating scale form, 40
  interviewing, 14
  need for, 15–16
  recruiting, 12
  role of, 2–3
  and teachers, 37–38
  typical tasks of, 16–23
    clerical tasks, 16–18
    housekeeping tasks, 18–19
    instruction-related tasks, 21–23